BEHIND THE SEEN

Larry

LICHTENWALTER

BEHIND THE SEEN

REVIEW AND HERALD® PUBLISHING ASSOCIATION
HAGERSTOWN, MD 21740

The author assumes full responsibility for the accuracy of all facts
and quotations as cited in this book.

Unless otherwise noted, Scripture quotations are from the *New American Standard Bible,*
© The Lockman Foundation 1960, 1962, 1963, 1968, 1971, 1972, 1973, 1975, 1977.
Scripture quotations identified CEV are from the Contemporary English Version.
Copyright © American Bible Society 1991, 1995. Used by permission.
Texts credited to Clear Word are from *The Clear Word,* copyright © 1994 by Jack Blanco.
Texts credited to NEB are from *The New English Bible.* © The Delegates of the Oxford
University Press and the Syndics of the Cambridge University Press 1961, 1970. Reprinted
by permission.
Texts credited to NIV are from the *Holy Bible, New International Version.* Copyright © 1973,
1978, 1984, International Bible Society. Used by permission of Zondervan Bible Publishers.
Texts credited to NKJV are from the New King James Version. Copyright © 1979,
1980, 1982 by Thomas Nelson, Inc. Used by permission. All rights reserved.
Bible texts credited to NRSV are from the New Revised Standard Version of the
Bible, copyright © 1989 by the Division of Christian Education of the National Council of
the Churches of Christ in the U.S.A. Used by permission.
Verses marked TLB are taken from *The Living Bible,* copyright © 1971 by Tyndale
House Publishers, Wheaton, Ill. Used by permission.

This book was
Edited by Gerald Wheeler
Copyedited by Delma Miller and James Cavil
Interior design by Tina Ivany
Cover design by Willie Duke
Electronic makeup by Shirley M. Bolivar
Typeset: 12/15 Bembo

PRINTED IN U.S.A.

05 04 03 02 01   5 4 3 2 1

R&H Cataloging Service
Lichtenwalter, Larry Lee, 1952–
    Behind the seen

    1. Bible. OT. Esther—Criticism, interpretation, etc.   I. Title.

                         222.9

ISBN 0-8280-1511-2

DEDICATED TO

my friend and mentor Miroslav Kis,
who has taught me to see beyond the visible
and to live for the unseen

CONTENTS

INTRODUCTION: THE QUEEN AND I 9

AN UPSIDE-DOWN CAKE 13
Esther 9:1-5

LIFESTYLES OF THE RICH AND FAMOUS 27
PLUS—BEAUTY AND THE FEAST
Esther 1:1-12

MR. LONELY AND THE PRETENDER 40
Esther 2:1-18

IF YOU UNDERSTAND THIS, YOU'RE IN TROUBLE 52
Esther 2:21-3:6

THIS IS YOUR HOUR. STAND! SPEAK! DIE! 65
JUST DON'T BE SILENT
Esther 4:1-16

SACRED HOOPS—WHEN BEING AWARE IS MORE 79
IMPORTANT THAN BEING SMART
Esther 4:13-5:5

WHEN LIFE ISN'T FAIR AND HONOR IS YOUR SHAME 93
Esther 5:9-6:3

WHEN THE END JUSTIFIES THE BEAMS 109
Esther 7:1-10

HANG 10—ENOUGH IS NOT ENOUGH 126
Esther 9:1-17

A PUR-FECT DAY FOR A FOREVER PARTY 141
Esther 9:20-32

EPILOGUE 154
THE PILGRIM SOUL IN YOU
Esther 10:1-3

THE QUEEN AND I

My affair with Esther started rather unexpectedly and abruptly. She hadn't even crossed my mind for who knows how long. Years, perhaps. Until that day she suddenly inflamed my imagination so much that my heart couldn't let her go and I found myself compelled to pursue her with a passion. But the relationship later left me confused and wary of any more dealings with her.

It was one of those Sabbaths during which I was spectator rather than preacher—a watcher from the back row. As I sat listening a couple hundred elementary school young people and their teachers conducted a special Christian education worship service. The inspiring program was the kind that declares, "Yes, Christian education is worth the investment!"

Unfortunately the program had a lot of dead time between choirs, band pieces, skits, and readings. The transitions seemed unnecessarily awkward and drawn out. So I flipped my Bible open and started reading Esther. She just happened to be there.

Since I was just filling time, it was all rather unplanned and aimless. Or so I thought. But when she emerged from the pages, I knew that I couldn't let her go. As one scene leaped to the next in the rapidly unfolding drama, a voice inside kept saying, "Preach me! Preach me!" Nearly every episode in the Esther epic overflowed with subtle moral and spiritual implications that I had never noticed before. The relevance of the issues for our postmodern time-of-the-end generation lit a fire in my heart. By the end of the church service I had finished the book. I literally could not put Esther down. My imagination had awakened in new directions, and I felt compelled to do something about it. So I prayed, "OK, Lord, I will push aside my planned fall sermon series (for which I had already spent a couple hundred dollars on books and done some serious study toward) and develop Esther instead."

Then my problems began.

You see, you find some things about Esther to love or admire, but many other things about her leave you scratching your head. Even uneasy.

You love the story—it's hard not to. An orphaned girl raised in Persia by a cousin named Mordecai becomes the wife of the celebrated King Xerxes by winning the Miss Persia contest.

It's a touching rags-to-riches romance. But one that quickly turns sinister when Haman, Xerxes' right-hand man—a raging Nazi who would like nothing better than to annihilate the Jews—convinces the king to let him exterminate all the Jews in the empire and confiscate their property.

That's where Esther comes in—literally. She takes a chance and pops into the king's office without an appointment—something that could get her head chopped off for. She wears her royal robes and stands at the door. Xerxes likes what he sees and summons her in. One invitation leads to another, and by the time she has finished hosting a couple elegant private banquets for just Xerxes and Haman, the king not only agrees to call off the ethnic cleansing but orders Haman to be hung on the very gallows he had prepared for Mordecai.

Aside from being beautiful, Esther was a gutsy woman. You have to admire her courage. She's a woman of strength and dignity.

But you find some things hard to understand; things that make you downright uneasy. Just to name a couple, such as why she didn't want to tell anyone about her belief in the God of Israel. Or how steely and unbending—even harsh—she appears when she shows no mercy by asking that Haman's 10 sons be hoisted up on the gallows to rot and be picked apart by the birds.

The careful reader finds Esther filled with a host of moral entanglements and seeming compromises with contemporary culture. One isn't sure what to think. Why would she consent to marry a Zoroastrian in the first place? What about all those drinking parties? Or all the killing? The sex and the sexism? How Persian did Esther look or act? What did Esther do or not do? How is she an example of what God's people are to do? How does she illustrate what they must never do? And where's God in all this? He never appears in the entire book. Is He hiding? Is Esther just another product of history? Is the book of

Esther an example of the cultural conditioning of Scripture, how its words are merely human ones—the thoughts of an ancient people who understood God in light of a civilization remote from our own?

When you read Esther the familiar becomes strange. Some things are tough to figure out. You scratch your head and wonder, "Is this the Esther I've known? Surely not!"

That was my dilemma—reconciling the Esther I had known with the one now emerging from the text. By the time I had read the book through in various translations, reviewed several commentaries on Esther, and studied key passages in the Hebrew, I had decided that Esther was a hot potato too difficult for me to handle. Three Esthers now stood in front of me, each suggesting a different interpretation of the book. I kept praying, "Will the real Esther please stand up!" (Remember the "To Tell the Truth" game show?) I wanted to drop her and run! To get on with something else—something safer.

But I didn't! I kept her. And as with any relationship, the more time you spend with someone the more you come to see what the person is all about.

My discomfort turned to passion again as I discovered in this enigmatic little book things most of us haven't stopped to think about for a long time. Things *behind the seen* of our lives and our enchanting yet intimidating world—including an incredible picture of God and how He is working right now to awaken us to the issues of our final generation. Esther is an epic rich in ethics and eschatology (last things) that can set afire our imagination about God and His last-day people.

Perhaps Esther hasn't crossed your mind for a long time. Maybe you've read the book and come away wondering what it all meant or even not sure if she's worth the read at all. Perchance you've never looked into her pages at all. Whatever, I can guarantee you one thing: If you take the half hour or so to read her story in the Bible, then journey with me in this book for a while, you won't want to quit. By the time you reach the end it will have awakened your imagination in new ways about what's going on *behind the seen*. And hopefully a new fire will burst into flame in your heart for the God who works behind the seen for you.

CHAPTER ONE

AN UPSIDE-DOWN CAKE

Esther 9:1-5

Pineapple upside-down cake was always one of my childhood favorites. The soft-textured yellowy cake—covered with candied pineapple circles swimming in a rich caramel syrup with bright-red maraschino cherries set in each center—delighted both my eyes and my mouth. Somehow, one piece never satisfied. Mostly, though, I remember being fascinated by the mystery of it all. Upside-down cakes are one of life's subtle mysteries. That which we normally expect to be on the top ends up on the bottom, and that which is typically found on the bottom rises to the top. My young mind always wondered about that. *This isn't the way it's supposed to be!* I thought. *But it sure looks good. And tastes great!*

In the days of Queen Esther the Medo-Persian Empire was like an upside-down cake. The enemies of God's people had hoped to overpower and destroy them. Those enemies were like the batter of the upside-down cake that submerged and threatened to eradicate the tasty fruit—God's people. On Adar 13 and 14, however, the "baking" period ended and, like the cake, the empire was turned right side up to the enjoyment of all.[1]

Esther is the story of how anti-Jewish forces in the Medo-Persian Empire enacted an irrevocable decree to inflict death on the Jews of the empire. "Then the king's scribes were summoned on the thirteenth day of the first month, and it was written just as Haman commanded. . . . Letters were sent by couriers to all the king's provinces to destroy, to kill, and to annihilate all the Jews, both young and old, women and children, in one day, the thirteenth day of the twelfth month, which is the month of Adar, and to seize their possessions as plunder" (Esther 3:12, 13).

For two months those opposed to the Jews were able to anticipate, perhaps relish, the day when they could wipe out the Jews once and for all and plunder their property. All that delight suddenly evaporated, though, when another irrevocable decree allowed the Jews to protect themselves. "The king granted the Jews who were in each and every city the right to assemble and to defend their lives, to destroy, to kill, and to annihilate the entire army of any people or province which might attack them, including children and women, and to plunder their spoil" (Esther 8:11).

In the months leading up to Adar 13, fear so filled the hearts of many non-Jews that they converted to Judaism (verse 17). And Adar 13 witnessed a dramatic shift of power. "Now in the twelfth month (that is, the month of Adar), on the thirteenth day when the king's command and edict were about to be executed, on the day when the enemies of the Jews hoped to gain the mastery over them, it was turned to the contrary so that the Jews themselves gained the mastery over those who hated them" (Esther 9:1). A dread literally immobilized the enemies of God's people to such a degree that they were unable to defend themselves. In the end, they were destroyed and God's people triumphed (verses 1-10).

The cake was turned right side up. An unexpected reversal and the making of a great party filled with feasting and rejoicing (verse 17), it was a dream come true!

Some have suggested that we can sum up the theme of the entire book of Esther in two Hebrew words—*nahăpôk hû'*—"the reverse occurred" (verse 1).[2] One of the most notable characteristics of the story of Esther is "reversal." Reversal comes when an action or a state of affairs intended or expected to produce a certain result ironically leads to the exact opposite outcome. The book explicitly states the principle of reversal: "The tables were turned and the Jews got the upper hand" (verse 1, NIV).[3]

Furthermore, every major character in the story of Esther experienced some kind of unexpected reversal of fortune. Vashti was Ahasuerus's most beautiful queen, a woman of dignity, power, and moral virtue, but the king demoted her to the ignominious status of one of the king's untouchable concubines, never to see his face again

(Esther 1:19). Esther was an inconsequential orphan who became the celebrated queen of one of the world's most powerful empires (Esther 2:7, 17). The secret plan of Bigthan and Teresh to murder King Ahasuerus resulted in their own inglorious death by public hanging (verses 19-23).

The two leading characters, Haman and Mordecai, also experienced reversal. Haman received the king's prestigious signet ring only to have it taken away (Esther 3:10; 8:2). He conspired to exterminate the Jews and wound up begging a Jew for his life (Esther 3:6; 7:7). After building a gallows to hang Mordecai on, he perished on it himself (Esther 5:14; 7:10). At one point in the story we find Mordecai dressed in sackcloth and covered with ashes (Esther 4:1-3). Later he found himself in glorious royal robes of blue and white (Esther 6:10, 11; 8:15). The story begins with Mordecai sitting at the king's gate as a low-level official (Esther 2:19; 3:2), but ends with Mordecai as Medo-Persia's prime minister (Esther 10:3).

Even non-Jews in the city of Susa swung from bewilderment to shouts of joy (Esther 3:15; 8:15). The king and his courtiers who would have kept their women under control wound up following the dictates of or taking their cues from a woman in power (Esther 1:12-22; 9:12). Ultimately, all the exiled people of God living in the Medo-Persian Empire experienced the exhilarating moment of unexpected reversal. Interestingly, "the very structure of Esther suggests the transformation 'from a time of grief to one of joy, and from an occasion of mourning to a holiday.'"[4] "Because on those days the Jews rid themselves of their enemies, and it was a month which was turned for them from sorrow into gladness and from mourning into a holiday" (Esther 9:22).

Something's Missing

So the people of God experienced an unexpected reversal of fortunes, a surprising turn of events. The cake turned right side up as the life-and-death crisis all worked out far better than anyone might have dared to imagine. But why? How?

On the surface of it, the unfolding narrative in chapter 9 suggests three possible answers. First, the cake turned right side up when the people of God took a stand and defended themselves (Esther 9:1, 5; 8:11, 13). In other words, we can solve life's dilemmas or meet formidable crises in our own strength. All we have to do is stand up for our rights and speak out, as Esther did. By presenting a united and formidable front, we can fight for ourselves, as the Jews did.

Second, the cake became right side up when the people of God received assistance from sympathetic friends (Esther 9:3). Undoubtedly there come those overwhelming moments when we are powerless to meet life's emergencies by ourselves, so we must look to the world around for help. At times the people of God need the people of the world to get things done. The state or technology or methodology or ideology—the people of the world—are crucial in turning the tide when someone is being exploited or threatened.

Finally, the cake flipped right side up when the enemies of God's people felt a dread of them (verse 2). Dread? Being afraid of? Yeah, much of life is a mind game. Whoever defines reality wins. So strut your stuff. Act big. Flex your muscles. Intimidate your enemy with blustery talk. Take some aggressive stance or offensive action. Litigate. Hurl verbal or written threats. Whisper behind the scene. Do whatever it takes to unnerve them or to get to where they are afraid to follow through with their sinister design against you.

So stand up for yourself, get help from your friends, or thrust your chest out and create such an aura about you that your enemies quake. Here are three ways you can turn the cake right side up. But where is God in all this?

Surprisingly, nowhere does the book of Esther explicitly say that the cake turned right side up because God intervened in behalf of His people. In fact, it appears that the meaning of the Hebrew words used to describe this unimaginable reversal is that the Jews "themselves" did it.[5] Several modern translations interpret it this way. "It was turned to the contrary so that the Jews *themselves* gained the mastery over those who hated them" (verse 1). "Because on those days the Jews rid *themselves* of their enemies" (verse 22).

But where's God in all this?

One of the most frustrating things in life involves looking for something you know you have but can't find. One time I was working on a project at my computer at home, books and papers stacked all around me. At one point I was unable to find a thin little book I had just quoted from. Although I scoured my study, I couldn't find it. Round and round my desk I went, looking on the floor, under papers, between stacks of books, from shelf to shelf in my library, in drawers, but to no avail. I even went upstairs thinking I may have carried it there during a break. Still no book. So I reluctantly went back to work without it—frustrated, still wondering, *Where in the world is that book? I just had it!* A few moments later I picked up the Bible that lay open on the table next to my computer and, would you believe, there it was right in front of me. It had been there the whole time. Yet I had looked there—or so I thought.

Our frustration in searching in vain for something that is literally right under our nose is the same as that experienced by the reader of the book of Esther. Where is God hiding? Nowhere does the book mention God, or even hint at Him, in any of its 10 chapters.[6] The narrative mentions the Persian king 190 times in 167 verses, but God not once.[7] In fact, Esther is the only one of the 66 books of the Bible that does not explicitly name God.[8] The book records no prayer offered in God's name. Not a single individual says, "God is here!" No one gives Him the credit for Haman's hanging, Esther's becoming queen, Mordecai's promotion, or the saving of the Jews from genocide. Nor does God seem to say in any clear way throughout the book, "I am God. I am in charge. I'm working these things out. I've taken charge." God is absolutely invisible, apparently absent.

This lack of any explicit reference to God in the story of Esther seems to be deliberate.[9] The disturbing shift from God to human ingenuity and power gives the impression that life's events and their results are ultimately under the control of resourceful human beings.[10] That we are the ones who shape and modify our lives and determine the course of history. It's our ingenuity, our intelligence, our power that turns the cake right side up. On the surface, Esther seems humanistic, projecting a kind of "do-it-yourself" approach to life.

Interestingly, that is exactly how many of the exiled Jews living in the time of Esther actually felt. "God has abandoned us," they said to themselves. "He is either unwilling or not able to act in our behalf. We have to go it alone." The destruction of their city and Solomon's glorious Temple by Nebuchadnezzar's armies, followed by decades of humiliating exile, threatened the very foundations of their religious convictions. God seemed absent, detached, uninvolved. The horizontal perspective was all they could see. Most of the Jewish exiles living in the Persian Empire dwelled in the flatlands with, as Solomon would say in Ecclesiastes, a narrow, nothing-new-under-the-sun view of life and reality. "This is all there is to life and we're alone. All we have is ourselves and our resourcefulness. God is nowhere to be found."

Not surprisingly, after all that happened to the Jews during the Holocaust, the absence of God in Esther makes the book very much alive for contemporary secular Jews.[11] "We know what that's like!" they say. As did their ancestors in Persian exile, contemporary Jews understand what it means to ask, "Where's God?" and find only silence. For many modern Jews the story of Esther "adds up to a lesson in monumental good luck—a lesson supremely relevant, supremely painful, for a Jewish 'generation' after a time of monumental bad luck."[12] Post-Holocaust Jewish theologian Fackenheim suggests that "after what has happened . . . Esther is strange no more. What if this once-strange book in the Jewish Bible had to be moved from the periphery to the centre, so as to provide the new principle uniting the whole? What if what once had been the repository of divine Revelation had now to become the classic repository of Jewish mythology, that is, for the Jews what the Homeric epics have been, all along, for the Greeks?"[13] "Could it be," he asks, "that the God of Israel and His promise to Israel, after all, are a myth which, like all myth, requires demythologisation; but that the myth needed to be believed by exiled Jews if they were to survive the exile?"[14]

"Whoa!" we say about such views of Esther or attitudes toward God. But in the thick of it, are we that much different? Don't we experience the agonizing silence of God in our own lives more than we would ever like? Or perhaps, it seems, God has been silent all our life. How do we feel, then, when the going is tough and the chips are down? When there's no way through the darkness? During such crises

18

of belief, aren't we tempted to think that "we" have to do something for ourselves, or secure the support of others, or put on a good show if anything is going to happen at all? Doesn't so much of life look like "monumental good luck" or "monumental bad luck"?

Living Somewhere Between

If you're not sure where God is when you read the book of Esther, you may be asking yourself the same question about those who profess to believe in God: Where is He in their lives? It comes as a surprise to the careful reader that neither Esther nor Mordecai—the principal characters in the book—gives any evidence of being particularly religious or spiritual—at least early on in the story.[15] We find Mordecai, a Jew, encouraging his young cousin (adopted daughter) Esther to marry a pagan king who was a zealous Zoroastrian,[16] knowing full well that should she fail in her highly unlikely bid to become queen, she would become a mere concubine lost in the king's harem till the day she died (Esther 2:8-14). Not only that, he commands her to hide, rather than reveal, her Jewish heritage and faith in God. "Don't tell anyone that you're a Jew. Don't tell anyone about your faith. Don't tell anyone about God." Esther dutifully obeys. She spends a year primping—bathing in oil, painting her face, learning what to wear—for that one erotic night with the king, hoping that she will be the one who satisfies him sexually and emotionally. Altogether, Esther hides her faith for nearly five years (Esther 2:16; 3:7). For the masquerade to last that long, she must have eaten,[17] dressed, and lived like a Persian. Perhaps she even worshiped like one with her husband on official occasions! Obviously very few knew who she really was. Only when her life was in danger did Esther come out of the closet.

Admittedly, that is not the way we're used to reading or thinking about Esther. So before you think about throwing this book down or sending me threatening mail for smearing your image of Esther as a godly woman of strength and dignity and prayer, we need some history.

The crisis in Esther partly resulted from the fact that God's people did not take advantage of the opportunity to leave Babylon and return to Jerusalem during more favorable times. On two occasions God graciously opened the way for His people to go back to Jerusalem. In the time of Cyrus only 50,000 or so out of the hundreds of thousands of captive Jews returned. The great majority of God's people chose to remain in the land of their exile rather than undergo the hardships of the return journey and the reestablishment of their desolated cities and homes. The same thing happened when Darius issued a second decree for the Jews in the Medo-Persian realm to return to the land of their fathers. During that opportunity the prophet Zechariah pleaded with the exiles to return, but to no avail: "'Ho there! Flee from the land of the north,' declares the Lord, 'for I have dispersed you as the four winds of the heavens,' declares the Lord. 'Ho, Zion! Escape, you who are living with the daughter of Babylon'" (Zech. 2:6, 7).

They just weren't interested. As Ronald Pierce writes, many "had forgotten their calling to separateness and had chosen to compromise their heritage for the sake of personal advancement."[18] The people of the Exile had only a halfhearted commitment to Jewish values and the God of heaven.

Ellen White concurs with this picture. She tells us that now, during the time of Esther, "the Jews who had failed of heeding the message to flee were called upon to face a terrible crisis. Having refused to take advantage of the way of escape God had provided, now they were brought face to face with death."[19]

Perhaps it explains Mordecai's and Esther's apparent willingness to compromise their relationship to the one true God. They, too, chose to live in exile away from the land of God's blessing. Mordecai, Esther, and the Jews of Susa were not only outside the Promised Land, they didn't seem all that concerned about God's program centered in that land.[20] They weren't interested in being a remnant who answered God's call, especially during a time of growing anti-Semitism (as the story of Esther demonstrates).

The story of Esther, then, is a narrative of marginal faith—or at best, floundering faith. It is a faith, perhaps, that is more a fact of birth than religious conviction. A faith evaded and hidden. The story of Esther points to the depth of the spiritual morass in which God's people had stumbled. That's why this book presents us with a host of moral entanglements and seeming compromises with contemporary culture. Esther is not as straightforward as Daniel and his friends of an earlier generation of exiles. You come away from the book with a lot of questions. What did Esther do or not do? Where is she an example of what God's people are to do? Where does she illustrate what they must never do?

I will not go so far as some do who say that Esther and Mordecai were downright unregenerate. That they didn't love the Lord or value His promises or care about their unique calling in the world. That by story's end we shouldn't consider them spiritual giants of faith.[21] After all, Ellen White refers to Esther as a Jew "who feared the Most High."[22] But where in the flow of events in this remarkable story does that statement apply?

What I will say is that there's a noticeable difference between how Esther and Mordecai behaved spiritually and morally at the beginning of the story and how they acted by the end. In a practical sense both Esther and Mordecai had given up their faith.[23] When confronted with the full reality of evil and its ominous plot to exterminate, though, Esther and Mordecai, together with other people of God, shook off their spiritual lethargy and rose to the occasion. They met the spiritual and moral challenge before it was too late! And when they did, as Ellen White writes, "God wrought marvelously for His penitent people."[24]

"Penitent people."

Those two words speak volumes. They unlock the meaning of this puzzling book and help us see what God was doing for and ultimately through His lukewarm, backsliden people. Esther is a story of God's awesome grace and sovereign compassion in spite of the spiritual lethargy and lack of vision among His people. And yet, through it all, He is the God backstage, the God *behind the seen*.

The God You're Looking For

We have three bathrooms in our house. One supposedly belongs to my wife and me. Tucked off our master bedroom, it's really out of the way. Notwithstanding, it seems that six of us use it. No matter how much you ask or plead or threaten, four sons, who have bathrooms of their own, invariably gravitate to our mirror, our toothpaste, our cotton swabs, Mom's brushes, Dad's Tinactin. Inevitably drawers get left open, towels dumped on the sink, or cotton swabs strewn on the floor.

One day I walked into our bathroom to find entire handprints glaring at me from the mirror. You couldn't miss the curling telltale patterns left by someone's greasy palms and fingers. "Who in the world has been in here now?" I mumbled out loud. "Why hands on the mirror? Couldn't they see the mess they left?"

I knew it wasn't our youngest son, since they were huge prints. Not being able to read fingerprints, though, at the most I could only interrogate suspects or bring hands back to the mirror for a fit. So there I was, trying to figure out who had thoughtlessly left their mark. One thing I knew for sure: someone had been in my bathroom.

God never appears in the entire book of Esther. But His actions and thoughts do. His plan does. In fact, His fingerprints are on every page. But His name never shows up.[25]

The book of Esther asks again and again as you read it, "Can you see His fingerprints?" Can you see God working even though it seems that everything is mere coincidence, monumental luck, or the result of human beings standing up for themselves or getting help from some other human source? That's the challenge each reader confronts—looking for the telltale fingerprints that affirm that God has been at work again.

Brenda was a young woman who wanted to learn rock climbing. Although she was scared of heights, she went with a group of her friends to climb a tremendous cliff. The rocky precipice was practically perpendicular. Brenda put on her gear, took hold of the rope, and with the help of others started up the face of that rock. Partway up she stopped on a ledge to catch her breath. As she was hanging there, whoever was holding the safety rope up at the top accidentally snapped it against Brenda's face, knocking out one of her contact lenses. Now, contact lenses are notorious for getting lost and almost impossible to find under ordinary circumstances, and here she was, hanging on a rock ledge with who knows how many hundreds of feet below her and hundreds of feet above her. Looking for the lens under these conditions seemed futile.

Far from home, Brenda was upset by the fact that she wouldn't be anywhere near a place where she could get a new lens. Her sight was now blurry and her weekend ruined. So she prayed that the Lord would help her find it. Maybe it was caught in the corner of her eye or dropped somewhere in her clothing or gear. Carefully she examined everyplace she could, but to no avail.

When Brenda reached the top, she asked a friend to look in the corner of her eye. Still no contact. Another search proved it wasn't in her clothing or gear either. As Brenda sat there looking across range after range of mountains, she thought of the verse of Scripture that says, "The eyes of the Lord run to and fro throughout the whole earth." "Lord," she prayed again, "You can see all these mountains. You know every single stone and leaf that's on those mountains, and You know exactly where my contact is. Please help me find it."

When the time came to leave, Brenda and her friends walked down the trail to the bottom. Just as they reached the base of the mountain, another party of rock climbers came along. As one of them started up the face of the cliff, he shouted, "Hey, guys! Anybody lose a contact lens?" Well, that would be startling enough, wouldn't it—the lost lens found under such implausible circumstances? God had answered her prayer. But you know how the guy climbing up the cliff found it? An ant was carrying that contact lens so that it was moving slowly across the face of the rock right in front of the climber's eyes. Rays of sunlight reflected dancing light beams as it moved along. He couldn't miss it! Imagine it. Stretching yourself out with your face pressed against the cliff, slowly inching your way upward, one crevice or bump at a time, and an ant comes strolling by carrying a contact lens. Awesome!

Now, Brenda's father is a cartoonist. When he heard this incredible story, he drew a picture of that ant lugging a contact lens held up high between its mandibles. Arising out from the ant's mind is one of those caption balloons with words in it: "Lord, I don't know why You want me to carry this thing. I can't eat it, and it's awfully heavy. But if this is what You want me to do, I'll carry it for You."

Obviously, Brenda and her family didn't just envision an ant going by with a contact lens in its mouth—they discerned the hand of God at work in a subtle but indisputable way.

When we take the coincidences and reversals in the book of Esther seriously, it is almost inescapable to conclude that the author wants us to believe, without being explicit, that God is in control of the course of history and the events of our lives.[26] When the cake turns right side up, we can be sure God is active and in control.

Chuck Swindoll writes that "in the mystery of God's timing, subtle things occur that the sensitive heart picks up. That's the role wisdom plays in life. Reading life's subtleties is what Christian maturity is all about."[27] The writer of Esther artfully assumes the perspective of the Jews during their disturbing postexilic experience. "If you observe carefully what has happened to us," he seems to say, "you would be able to detect God's presence with us."[28]

Surprisingly, the author uses the perceived absence of God to communicate a message of comfort and hope.[29] It is another reversal, the opposite of what we would expect. God's exiled people struggled with His apparent silence in their troubled lives. They felt abandoned and powerless against daunting circumstances. Many must have felt that their future totally depended upon their own actions. For some, it was simply in the hand of fate. With this in mind, the author of the book of Esther wanted to relieve the anxiety and loss of faith because of God's apparent continued silence in the midst of life's excruciating crises. He wanted to give them hope against the odds, assurance of divine assistance to meet the threat. That while there seemed to be only divine silence, God cared and would provide power to overcome. They could take courage to face the issues facing them head-on. As Michael Fox asserts, "when we scrutinize the text of Esther for traces of God's activity, we are doing what the author made us do. The author would have us probe the events we witness in our own lives in the same way."[30] "Where's God?" we ask so often. He's there! If you look just right, you can see Him.

How much we need that assurance!

Many are surprised to learn that the story of Esther has an eschatological dimension—a future orientation.[31] Its message speaks to every burning crisis God's people have met down through history, but will find its fullest expression in the end when the struggle between Christ and Satan heats up for one last conflict. Esther features both a cosmic as well as a personal individual dimension. Note the application specifically to end-time issues: "The trying experiences that came to God's people in the days of Esther were not peculiar to that age alone. The Revelator, looking down the ages to the close of time, has declared, 'The dragon was wroth with the woman, and went to make war with the remnant of her seed, which keep the commandments of God, and have the testimony of Jesus Christ.' Revelation 12:17. . . . The decree that will finally go forth against the remnant people of God will be very similar to that issued by Ahasuerus against the Jews. Today the enemies of the true church see in the little company keeping the Sabbath commandment, a Mordecai at the gate."[32]

Esther is a story for today. It has a message for God's end-time people and insight into the final crisis.

When we come to this book that never mentions God, we can actually see Him all the more profoundly and eloquently portrayed throughout it. He's there in invisible ink. In life we never see skywriting that says, "I'm here. You can count on Me." But by faith we detect Him and, inaudibly, we hear Him on a regular basis, reading Him written in the events of our lives—whether it be the crushing blows that drive us to our knees or the joyous triumphs that send our heart winging. When we pause long enough to look back, we can see His fingerprints.[33]

Where is the God we watch for when the going gets rough?

He is *behind the seen* working for our good even when we cannot see, or perhaps do not want to see, Him.[34]

He works providentially on behalf of His people despite their spiritual condition.[35]

He is an awesome God with incredible sovereign power.

He is absolutely invisible, yet always at work.

He is gracious toward His compromising people.

He cares for us.

What's more, He knows how to make great upside-down cake.

---

[1] A. Boyd Luter and Barry C. Davis, *God Behind the Seen: Expositions of the Books of Ruth and Esther* (Grand Rapids: Baker, 1995), pp. 322, 323.

[2] Jon D. Levenson, *Esther* (London: SCM Press, 1997), p. 8. The Niphal form of the verb *hāpak* means "to be reversed," "overturned," or "changed" (R. Laird Harris, ed., *Theological Wordbook of the Old Testament* [Chicago: Moody Press, 1980], vol. 1, pp. 221, 222).

[3] Angel Manuel Rodríguez, *Esther: A Theological Approach* (Berrien Springs, Mich.: Andrews University Press, 1995), p. 36.

[4] Levenson, pp. 8, 9.

[5] Luter and Davis, p. 324.

[6] "The author does not use traditional religious vocabulary; and, even more perplexing, the name of God and His titles are totally absent from the book" (Rodríguez, p. xi). See Luter and Davis, p. 99.

[7] John C. Whitcomb, *Esther: The Triumph of God's Sovereignty* (Chicago: Moody Press, 1979), p. 20.

[8] Luter and Davis, p. 100, n. 1.

[9] Rodríguez, p. 17.

[10] *Ibid.*, p. xi.

[11] Emil L. Fackenheim, *The Jewish Bible After the Holocaust: A Re-reading* (Manchester, England: Manchester University Press, 1990), pp. 60, 61.

[12] *Ibid.*, p. 62.

[13] *Ibid.*

[14] *Ibid.*, p. 65.

[15] Luter and Davis, pp. 100, 101; Whitcomb, pp. 23-28.

[16] Whitcomb, p. 23. Some 40 years later Nehemiah, writing perhaps to the children of the Jews of Esther's time, issues a scathing indictment against the practice of mixed marriages (Neh. 13:23-27).

[17] It is possible that the favors Hegai showered on Esther included kosher food (Esther 2:9). The text, however, is not clear in this matter. It appears most consistent that the reference to "cosmetics and foods" simply refers to the fact that life in the harem may not have been all that comfortable for the newcomer or second-rate and that the more favored fared better.

[18] As quoted in Luter and Davis, p. 102.

[19] Ellen G. White, *Prophets and Kings* (Mountain View, Calif.: Pacific Press Pub. Assn., 1917), p. 600.

[20] Whitcomb, p. 26.

[21] See Whitcomb, pp. 26, 27; Luter and Davis, pp. 363-366.

[22] White, p. 601.

[23] Jon Paulien, *Present Truth in the Real World* (Boise, Idaho: Pacific Press Pub. Assn., 1993), p. 78.

[24] White, p. 602.

[25] Max Lucado, *Life Lessons From the Inspired Word of God—Books of Ruth and Esther* (Waco, Tex.: Word Publishing, 1996), p. 43.

[26] Rodríguez, p. 38.

[27] Charles R. Swindoll, *Esther: A Woman of Strength and Dignity* (Nashville: Word Publishing, 1997), p. 129.

[28] Rodríguez, pp. 97, 98.

[29] *Ibid.*, p. 96.

[30] Michael V. Fox, *Character and Ideology in the Book of Esther* (Columbia, S.C.: University of South Carolina Press, 1991), p. 247.

[31] Rodríguez, p. 107.

[32] *Ibid.*, p. 605.

[33] Swindoll, p. 17.

[34] Luter and Davis, p. 103.

[35] *Ibid.*, p. 366.

CHAPTER TWO

LIFESTYLES OF THE RICH AND FAMOUS PLUS—BEAUTY AND THE FEAST

Esther 1:1-12

In the days of Ahasuerus, the Ahasuerus who ruled from India to Ethiopia, a hundred and twenty-seven provinces. At this time he sat on his royal throne in Susa the capital city. In the third year of his reign he gave a banquet for all his officers and his courtiers; and when his army of Persians and Medes, with his nobles and provincial governors, were in attendance, he displayed the wealth of his kingdom and the pomp and splendour of his majesty for many days, a hundred and eighty in all. When these days were over, the king gave a banquet for all the people present in Susa the capital city, both high and low; it was held in the garden court of the royal pavilion and lasted seven days. There were white curtains and violet hangings fastened to silver rings with bands of fine linen and purple; there were alabaster pillars and couches of gold and silver set on a mosaic pavement of malachite and alabaster, of mother-of-pearl and turquoise. Wine was served in golden cups of various patterns: the king's wine flowed freely as befitted a king, and the law of the drinking was that there should be no compulsion, for the king had laid it down that all the stewards of his palace should respect each man's wishes. In addition, Queen Vashti gave a banquet for the women in the royal apartments of King Ahasuerus" (Esther 1:1-9, NEB).

The opening verses of Esther reveal the massive extent of King Ahasuerus's[1] political power and his great wealth. Like the behind-the-scenes stories of the rich and famous, they offer an inside look at a lifestyle of pomp and extravagance difficult for most of us to even imagine. You can't read them without being impressed. Wealth, power, fame, and a beautiful spouse—the proverbial money, sex, and power—what more could anyone want? As ruler of the Medo–Persian Empire, King Ahasuerus had all of this and much more. At the time Esther's story begins, he was only in the third of his 21-year reign (485-465 B.C.). The most powerful ruler of his day, the boundaries of his kingdom reached as far as Pakistan in the east to the northern part of modern Sudan in the west—encompassing nearly 2 million square miles. His winter/spring capital at Susa was a garden paradise abounding in fruits and flowers, surrounded by streams and mountains. His palace complex rose 120 feet above the city, further announcing his majestic grandeur.

In the midst of such a luxurious environment, Ahasuerus threw an extravagant banquet that lasted 180 days (verse 4)—six full months of partying. The Hebrew word for banquet literally means "drinking feast." No ordinary bash, it was 180 days of loud music, wild dancing, lots of food, all the booze you could handle, and . . . *guided tours.* The purpose of the extravaganza appears in the simple Hebrew word *ra'ah* ("to display")—"when he displayed the riches of his royal glory and the splendor of his great majesty" (verse 4). The form of the Hebrew verb places emphasis on causing someone to look at or gaze on something so intently that it leaves a deep, lasting impression on the imagination. King Ahasuerus wanted the leaders of his kingdom—princes, nobles, and military leaders—to get a feel for the vast wealth of his domain. He desired for them to ooh and aah at his own personal splendor. Ahasuerus flaunted his wealth and splendor during a half year of feasting for one reason and one reason alone—to impress the people of his world with his greatness.

Then, if that wasn't enough, Ahasuerus threw another seven-day "private" outdoor party for all the residents of Susa and for everyone else present in the city at the time (verse 5). Once again, the drinks were on the house, but this time they were "served in goblets of gold, each one different from the other" (verse 7, NIV). In the garden court of his royal pavilion "there were white curtains and violet hangings fastened to silver rings with bands of fine linen and purple; there were alabaster pillars and couches of gold and silver set on a mosaic pavement of malachite and alabaster, of mother-of-pearl and turquoise" (verse 6,

NEB). This long exclamation-like sentence creates a mass of images that purposely overwhelm the sensory imagination. Here we get a glimpse into the physical beauty and sensual pleasure Ahasuerus's wealth was able to produce. Evidently the immensity of the king's fortune was such that, even after being on exhibition for 180 days, its glory and majesty remained undiminished. Ahasuerus's riches made such a lasting impression that the book of Esther recorded them years after the event. Some items were so impressive that time could not blur the detail in people's memory.[2] Yes, it was a celebration of a lifetime— a banquet to remember.

By the way, historians tell us that when the Spartans thoroughly defeated Ahasuerus, they found in the spoil of the camp tents covered with gold and silver, golden couches, bowls and cups, and even gold and silver kettles. If Ahasuerus took that much gold and silver with him when he went to battle, we can only imagine what he left behind in his palaces and storehouse. It must have been incredible.[3]

A House of Cards

My family played a lot of cards when I was a boy. They'd gather around the kitchen table on a Saturday night playing pinochle or poker with friends. Most of the time we kids just hung around eating ice cream and pretzels, playing hide-and-seek outdoors, or watching TV. We weren't much interested in playing cards. Sometimes, though, we did play *with* cards. We'd build elaborate card houses. The challenge came in building the biggest house, the most elaborate structure. It was a lot of fun. You had to balance the cards just right, though. Only gravity and balance held it all together. Once you had that foundation, you would gingerly add more cards here and there, each dependent upon the support of the other. We'd lay layers of card upon card to create an elaborate but fragile house of cards. The slightest movement, though, could send the whole thing crumbling. Even when we succeeded in building a house that held together long enough for us to show it off and explain its grand features, it would always be just a house of cards.

Everything the book of Esther has been telling us about King Ahasuerus thus far is a generous layering of card upon card to create an elaborate but fragile "house of cards."[4] Now someone shakes the table. It's the last night of the party. The king is drunk. And in his inebriated state he decides to show off one more of his greatest prizes. He calls for Queen Vashti to come with her royal crown "in order to display her beauty to the people and the princes, for she was beautiful" (verse 11). There's that word "display" again. No doubt it took the form of parading her, perhaps scantily dressed, before those who would have nothing in mind but lust. "Hey, everyone, look, enjoy . . . envy. On top of everything you've seen the past six months, I've got really great sex, too!"

But Vashti refuses. Immediately the true character of the king bursts through. The terse biblical record is a real eye-opener—he "became very angry and his wrath burned within him" (verse 12). After 180 days of one party, and six days of another very successful party, Ahasuerus was not planning on it ending this way. But it did. His party ruined on a disconcertingly personal level, he was livid.

Suddenly the king is not as powerful as he first appears to be.[5] Someone actually disobeys him—and in public, no less. The house of cards crumbles. Now the scene changes from "Lifestyles of the Rich and Famous" to the "Private Lives of Public People." We move behind the "seen" to what's really there. Verses 10-12 form the fulcrum point in the unfolding narrative. From here on we see just how empty the exalted king and his mighty kingdom really are. In fact, the next scene is a bunch of drunken men running around worried that they will lose control of their wives (verses 13-22). Ahasuerus has summoned his most trusted wise men for advice—shakers and movers such as Carshena, Shethar, Admatha, Tarshish, Meres, Marsena, and Memucan (verses 13, 14). "What am I gonna do now?" he asks with an agitated voice. "What does the law say I should do to Vashti because she didn't obey my command?" (see verse 15).

Memucan describes their predicament well: "The queen's conduct will become known to all the women causing them to look with contempt on their husbands by saying, 'King Ahasuerus commanded Queen Vashti to be brought into his presence, but she did not come.' And this day the ladies of Persia and Media who have heard of the queen's conduct will speak in the same way to all the king's princes, and there will be plenty of contempt and anger" (verses 17, 18).

Can't you hear this drunken all-men's gathering muttering and mumbling, "Oh no. What do we do now? When my wife hears about this, there'll be no controlling her then." And on and on and on. In the end the domestic problem between the king and his wife gets blown all out of proportion and affects all the marriages in the empire. Memucan spins it all in such a way that they now see disobedience of wives to their husbands as dangerous to the peace and security of the state. When all is said and done, Vashti gets deposed and women throughout the empire come under an irrevocable royal edict to show due respect to their husbands and treat them—according to the Hebrew word *yeqār*—as priceless or magnificent treasures, whether they are great or small (verses 20-22).

From our postmodern perspective, it all may seem like old-boy bigoted politically incorrect overkill, but drunken party or not, it was serious business. Sadly, though, it was no small business either in the eyes of every woman in the empire as well. No matter the culture, or the times, or the sociological context, it still hurt. It was still demeaning.

Before we go on, I want us to catch a very important perspective that helps us understand what's taking place in this first chapter. The opening verses of the book of Esther clearly move from the universal (the gigantic empire extending from Pakistan to Sudan) to the more limited (the royal throne in the capital city) to the individual (King Ahasuerus himself).[6] Also, the book zooms in chronologically from the third year of his reign, to a six-month period, to a single week, and finally, to a particular day in his life and what takes place on that specific day (verses 3, 4, 5, 10). The author identifies for us the very center of the Medo-Persian Empire's power and psyche.[7] Everything is collapsing, and what we see happening with the king mirrors what the whole Persian world is like. The king and what he does characterize the empire as a whole. At the center of the empire, he is its throbbing pulse. Personifying the glory of human achievement expressed in Medo-Persian culture, he represents his culture's values, priorities, character, and its way of thinking and acting (moral perspective and behavior). When we see the king and what he does on a particular day in a particular situation, we are to see the larger world for what it really is.

What kind of world does the story of Esther portray? First, the book of Esther depicts a world running headlong into foolish distraction, one caught up with "the good life." Absorbed with materialism and enamored with outward beauty and self-indulgence, it loves extravagance, applause, and power—a world of appearances.

Second, Esther projects a dysfunctional world navigating with a faulty moral compass. Remember, King Ahasuerus characterizes Medo-Persia's moral/spiritual compass. A character study of Esther's Ahasuerus leaves one with the image of a leader obsessed with honor and materialism. Self-indulgent, impulsively generous, and unable to say no, he is a nice guy who abdicates responsibility and surrenders effective power to those who know how to push the right buttons. Ahasuerus is also a lazy thinker. He does not like to spend energy on thought—the moral implications of decisions—so people can get their way by doing his thinking for him. As a result, he often acts without quite knowing what he is getting himself into, or what the consequences of certain things might be. Each time the king abdicated thought to those with more energy for such things, it led to moral tragedy. Failure to think was the king's most dangerous flaw.[8] Ahasuerus is an incredible picture of ineffective leadership. The book of Esther thus presents a dysfunctional world navigating with a faulty moral compass.

During the Monica Lewinsky scandal many of the American people rationalized away President Clinton's behavior even after they suspected, and later knew, he was lying. Because the economy was strong, millions of people said that infidelity in the Oval Office was just a private affair—something between the president and Hillary. We heard it time and time again during those months: "As long as the president is doing a good job, it's nobody's business what he does with his personal life." Again and again people said, "Character doesn't matter." That "there is an important distinction between public and private character. What candidates do in private is largely irrelevant. What matters is their public conduct."[9]

Samuel Adams would disagree. In a letter to James Warren, written November 4, 1775, Adams asserts: "He who is void of virtuous attachments in private life, is, or very soon will be, void of all regard for his country. There is seldom an instance of a man guilty of betraying his country who had not before lost the feeling of moral obligation in his private connections."

Finally, the story of Esther sketches a moody, oppressive world that coerces its own brand of morality. History remembers Ahasuerus for his rage (Esther 1:12; 7:7). When his brother's wife refused his sexual advances, Ahasuerus seduced her daughter and then arranged the murder of the entire family.[10] On another occasion, when a storm destroyed a bridge that he had commanded built, he called for the heads of the bridge-building engineers.[11] The name Ahasuerus would send a shiver down the spine of anyone potentially at odds with his will. He was, by reputation and by deed, a king to fear. Furthermore, as an extension of fallen humanity, the Persian Empire was inherently anti-God and therefore naturally in opposition to the people of God.

Vashti's decision, and subsequent removal, point to a world that may well exact a price from those who take a personal stand for what is morally right.[12] Interestingly, the image the book of Esther presents here is one in which the men—who are in power—are the ones who are both immoral and oppressive, while the women—who obviously have lesser social status—are both moral and oppressed. It makes me think of Madonna Kolbenschlag's cutting words: "The ancient world debated the question, 'Can women be saved?' Today many women are asking the question, 'Can men be saved?' They ask this in a much more profound way: can men develop the behaviors that the future of the family, society, and the world seem to require? . . . Perhaps the churchmen who once told us that 'women will be saved in childbearing' (1 Tim. 2:15) will have to revise the instruction. Perhaps men will now be saved by child-caring."[13]

What we at first see about the great Medo-Persian Empire and her remarkable king appears magnificent, overwhelming, grand. But it's all a fragile house of cards. Behind the seen we find emptiness. That's still our world!

Remember that classic Hans Christian Andersen tale "The Emperor's New Clothes"? The emperor was a vain little fellow who loved new clothes so much that he spent all his money on them. Nothing else mattered except showing himself off in new clothes. He had an outfit for every hour in the day. One day some swindlers came into town with a great idea. They promised to weave the emperor a new suit of clothing made of very special material that would be invisible to every person who was unfit for the office he held or who was exceptionally stupid. *Those must be valuable clothes,* thought the emperor. *By wearing them I will be able to discover which of the men in my empire are not fit for their posts. I will be able to distinguish wise men from fools. Yes, I must order clothes made from that special material right away.* And so he paid the swindlers a handsome sum of money in advance.

It was all a big fraud, of course. But the emperor's tailor and his own vanity so flattered and fooled him that the day came when he paraded through the streets stark naked. He believed he was wearing elegantly regal clothes when he had on nothing at all. All who saw him tried to deny what they were seeing. No one wanted to let it appear that he could see nothing. To do so would prove oneself stupid or not fit for his or her post. As you remember, the myth of the royal attire shattered when a little child—who didn't feel the need to impress those in positions of power—openly declared the emperor's nakedness. "But he has nothing on!"[14]

The author of the book of Esther is much like that little child. He allows the king to display his finery, his wealth, and his power to impress the people of his world with his assumed greatness. Then he systematically shows that seemingly powerful king to be quite powerless and morally bankrupt. The king's assumed greatness is mere empty display. What appears to be *the* preeminent mover and shaker in the eyes of the Medo-Persian Empire is in reality no more than water in the hands of the sovereign God.[15] As Proverbs says: "The king's heart is like channels of water in the hand of the Lord; He turns it wherever He wishes" (Prov. 21:1).

Here We Are

Right now you're probably thinking, *What in the world does all this have to do with me? Where does Esther come in to all this? Why are we spend-*

ing so much time on this part of the story? Isn't all this just background setting for the real action? No! This *is* the kind of world Esther and her people found themselves living in. The book of Esther unabashedly marvels at the glory of Persia and her remarkable king. In doing so it hints at the "sense of awe the Jewish exiles felt as they witnessed the magnificence of human achievement all around them."[16]

Why were they so reluctant to return to Jerusalem?

And why were they willing to hide their identity and compromise their faith?

Obviously, their gaze was on the glitzy display of power and glory in the Persian world around them. It all looked pretty desirable. Besides, the gigantic political monster called Medo-Persia was the sum and substance of what they knew as the civilized world. The exiled people of God were just peons in comparison with that great culture. It was only natural that they would feel intimidated. They were no-bodies in a world that glorified somebodies. On the face of it, it was the Medo-Persian Empire, not God, who was in control of the world. Either God was unwilling or incapable of helping His people. Or so they thought.

God's exiled people found themselves caught between being intimidated by their world on the one hand, and attracted to it on the other. That's where many of us often also stand today—awed, intimidated, attracted, overshadowed, enchanted, and threatened by our world. That can be particularly true in our post-Christian, postmodern culture.

God's Word appeals to us to "not love the world, nor the things in the world. If anyone loves the world, the love of the Father is not in him. For all that is in the world, the lust of the flesh and the lust of the eyes and the boastful pride of life, is not from the Father, but is from the world. And the world is passing away, and also its lusts; but the one who does the will of God abides forever" (1 John 2:15-17). But that's easier said than done. Sometimes all we see is "the seen." And when we or our God or our Adventist heritage or our blessed hope seems so insignificant in comparison to the gigantic monster we call the world, we give in. It's the tragic reality of many of God's professed people today.

The book of Esther would have us see our world as it really is—a mere house of cards. We need to look *behind the seen* and recognize:

That it is a house of cards that intimidates us.

That it is a house of cards that attracts us.

That it is a house of cards that threatens us.

That it is a house of cards that bewitches us.

That's it—just a house of cards. Period. End of story.

Esther will tell us, too, though, that even in a house of cards, ethics is still important. It is the foundation of true greatness, but you may pay a price for upholding it.

This is the world we're attracted to, intimidated by, feel insignificant against—unless we look *behind the seen* and discern its real moral spiritual core.

I believe Esther is calling us to examine our priorities and to be honest with ourselves. Could it be that we, too, are laying generous layer upon layer of cards to build our own house of cards?

It Is Here That God Works

My wife, Kathie, and I often take walks before we end our day. It's usually well after 10:00 p.m. before we get started—sometimes as late as midnight (such is the press of busy life). We have a two-mile routine around our country home that we either power-walk or just stroll along, depending on our mood. When we first step out of the porch light each night it's thick black. We can't see a thing. In fact, the harder we look, the blacker it gets. And if I disappear in the darkness first, Kathie has shrieked in frustration that she can't see me or know where I went. She's afraid I might scare her. So she frantically reaches in front of herself, hoping to touch my back or grab my shirt.

Once we hit the darkness, we search our memory for the angle of the driveway as it leaves the house and shuffle our feet for the feel of the asphalt. You can be sure that the couple times we have walked off the edge and our feet have hit the dry leaves of the forest floor we corrected our direction immediately. The picture of two intelligent mature grown-ups smacking into a tree trunk is humiliating. But usually by the time we hit the gravel at the end of the driveway the night sky offers some bearing. The uncanny thing is that in that mysterious darkness, you can see more from your peripheral vision, the edge of your eye, if you don't try to focus. You will see better if you look for the general rather than the specific, the outline rather than the detail—the silhouettes. And the amazing thing is that by the end of our walk that same darkness has shapes and depth and shadows filled with detail by the glow of the night sky even on a moonless night. I can even see my wife's eyes. Our kiss is never blind.

When I can't see God's form in the inky blackness, I need to give my eyes time to become accustomed to His way of working. The more I try to focus on Him, the less visible He seems to be. But if I just look out of the corner of my eye, let my peripheral vision survey the unknown, I will begin to see. First mere shadows, then a silhouette, and finally the details of His face.

The world that Esther portrays seems at first dark and absent of God. We detect only the human. As Charles Swindoll says, "all we've got so far is a huge gathering at a banquet and a drunken king and more than six months of revelry and the blatant display of carnal appetites by a bunch of insecure, frustrated men." [17] One would fear there's no one out there. But Esther would have us look for God at work in that very darkness. Let our eyes become accustomed to His way of working. Search for Him with our peripheral vision *behind the seen*.

We can't fall into the trap of thinking that God is asleep in our world, or that He is out of touch with drunken parties, or that He sits in heaven wringing His hands before godless leaders who make unfair, rash, or stupid decisions. God is always at work, but His ways are different than ours.

Ellen White tells us that "occasions of indulgence such as are pictured in the first chapter of Esther do not glorify God. But the Lord accomplishes His will through men who are nevertheless misleading others. . . . God impresses human minds to accomplish His purpose, even though the one used continues to follow wrong practices. . . . In His hand is the heart of every earthly ruler, to turn whithersoever He will, as He turneth the waters of the river. Through the experience that brought Esther to the Medo-Persian throne, God was working for the accomplishment of His purposes for His people. That which was done under the influence of much wine worked out for good to Israel."[18] God can even use occasions of indulgence.

I believe Vashti's refusal gives us a glimpse of God, too. She was brave enough to say no to what was blatantly wrong and took a moral stand against the greatest power in her world. Good for her! Her experience shows God at work in the hearts of people who don't even know Him. Vashti reminds us that in a world of money, sex, power, and applause, the foundation of true greatness is moral integrity. In doing so she opens the way for us to grasp a fundamental theme in Esther—when you disobey the king, when you run against the will of our world, when you stand for what is right, history will never be the same.[19] It's a moment during which God steps in and works His will. Think of it—every time someone resists the world's power, the course of history changes as God works. In the wake of Vashti's ethical stand, a vacancy opens up at the very top, in the king's household, and God has someone waiting in the wings to fill that opening. Little did Memucan realize that his suggestion, "Let the king give her royal position to another who is more worthy than she" (Esther 1:19), would become a thread of the divine tapestry.

In the midst of what's happening in our world, God's heart remains attached to His people, even when they are so often awed by the magnificence of human achievement and caught up with culture's glory, lifestyle, values, and worldview. It does not hinder God's plans when the events of our world are carnal or secular. Not only do we live in a world that is only a house of cards; it is the very world God works in. It is the world that God seeks to expose for all its emptiness, yet the very world that God sometimes uses to accomplish His perfect will for each one of us.

God is at work touching lives, shaping kingdoms. Whether you see Him or not, He is active in your life right now. Can you see His fingerprints?

---

[1] Scholars have positively indentified the biblical name Ahasuerus with the Persian Xerxes I.

[2] A. B. Luter and B. C. Davis, *God Behind the Seen,* p. 112.

[3] *Ibid.,* p. 111.

[4] *Ibid.,* p. 107.

[5] A. M. Rodríguez, *Esther: A Theological Approach,* p. 54.

[6] *Ibid.,* p. 46.

[7] *Ibid.,* pp. 46, 47.

[8] M. V. Fox, *Character and Ideology in the Book of Esther,* pp. 171-177.

[9] Jeremy Iggers, "Character: Is It Important, and If So, How?" Minneapolis *Star Tribune,* Oct. 25, 1992, p. 1A.

[10] Joyce G. Baldwin, *Esther: An Introduction and Commentary* (Downers Grove, Ill.: InterVarsity, 1984), pp. 18, 19, 55, 56.

[11] Luter and Davis, p. 109.

[12] Rodríguez, p. 53.

[13] Madonna Kilbenschlag, *Lost in the Land of Oz* (San Francisco: Harper and Row, 1988), pp. 73, 74.

[14] Hans Christian Andersen, "The Emperor's New Clothes," in William J. Bennett, ed., *The Book of Virtues* (New York: Simon and Schuster, 1993), pp. 630-634.

[15] Luter and Davis, p. 105.

[16] Eugene H. Merrill, "A Theology of Ezra-Nehemiah and Esther," in *A Biblical Theology of the Old Testament,* ed. Roy B. Zuck (Chicago: Moody Press, 1991), p. 203.

[17] C. R. Swindoll, *Esther: A Woman of Strength and Dignity,* p. 29.

[18] *The Seventh-day Adventist Bible Commentary,* Ellen G. White Comments, vol. 3, p. 1139.

[19] Rodríguez, p. 53.

CHAPTER THREE

MR. LONELY AND THE PRETENDER

Esther 2:1-18

In the winter of 1934 Navy admiral Richard Byrd lived for five months in a buried shack on the Ross Ice Barrier near the South Pole. The most honored explorer of his time, Byrd had come to collect weather data from that formidable environment. No person had ever ventured so far to the south or remained so long and lived to tell about it, for there on the surface of Ross Ice Barrier is the "coldest cold on the face of the earth."

The obstacles to the success of Byrd's mission were great. The temperature plummeted as low as 83 degrees below zero. Mountains of powdery, drifting snow threatened to entomb him in his little hovel. The Barrier terrain was a sheet of ice thousands of feet thick, and as level and featureless as the top of a kitchen table. And there was darkness. In mid-April the sun dropped below the horizon and did not return. By mid-May the only sunlight was a brief reddish glow low in the northern sky each day at noon. It was like "one layer of darkness piled on top of the other."

During those five months Byrd suffered from frostbite, stings from wind-blown pellets of sleet, carbon monoxide poisoning, lack of sleep, and malnutrition. He became lost in a blizzard during a foray from his shelter, and once nearly disappeared into a crevasse.

Yet when Byrd returned to civilization and wrote an account of his experience on the Barrier, the title of his account did not emphasize the terrain, the weather, the sickness, the danger, or the darkness. Rather it stressed the most fearfully devastating part of the entire winter. He called his book simply *Alone*.[1] Neither the winds, the great dunes of snow, the nausea, nor the long dense night could compare with the loneliness of being isolated from fellow human beings.

The second chapter of Esther plunges us straightaway into the lonely heart of the Persian king. "After these things when the anger of King Ahasuerus had subsided, he remembered Vashti and what she had done and what had been decreed against her" (Esther 2:1).

Nearly four years elapsed between the events recorded in chapter 1 and those in chapter 2. It was in the third year of his reign that Ahasuerus held the 180-day banquet (Esther 1:3). Esther became queen in his seventh year (Esther 2:16). History books tell us that in between those recorded events Ahasuerus launched an ambitious military campaign to conquer Greece. The land battle went quite well, but his vast armada of nearly 4,000 war vessels assembled at Salamis met a crushing defeat against a mere 271 Greek warships. Ahasuerus's navy perished like a school of fish caught in a net. He became dismayed and discouraged. So the phrase "after these things" (verse 1) involves more than what meets the eye of the casual reader. It includes the tragic events that took place after he had led an aborted expedition against Greece and returned to Susa in humiliating defeat.[2]

Ahasuerus entered his luxurious Susa palace weary of battle and dispirited by defeat. Disappointed with himself and humiliated, he longed for someone to greet him with arms outstretched. Someone who would offer words of comfort and understanding—not just a servant or one of his officers, but somebody who truly cared for him and his feelings. For the first time Ahasuerus knew true defeat and loneliness. It was the coldest of the cold, the darkness layered upon darkness of a long isolated stint on the Ross Ice Barrier.

In fact, Ahasuerus was desperate to find some comfort for his loneliness.[3] And all he could think of was Vashti (Esther 2:1). He remembered only her beauty, the warmth of her arms, the comfort of her understanding—and wished she were by his side once more.

That little Hebrew verb "remember" *(zākar)* often carries with it a note of compassion (see Gen. 40:14; Lev. 26:42, 45; Jer. 2). Its use here suggests that Ahasuerus has become melancholy in the absence of his wife Vashti and regretful of the severity of her punishment.[4] No longer drunk or angry, he thinks clearly now.

Now, the point is not that Ahasuerus simply needed a woman. Like other ancient monarchs, he had a harem full of them. With a snap of his finger she'd be in his presence, right there in his bedchamber. But Ahasuerus wasn't looking for a one-night stand. He wanted a wife. Someone to be near him through it all as his companion and who really cared.[5]

Apparently those closest to him recognized what was happening and knew they needed to do something quick about his depression. Any potential return of Vashti to power might mean their heads would roll, since it was they who had counseled the king to get rid of her in the first place. So they suggested a "find-a-bride" service. "Let a search be made for beautiful young virgins for the king. Let the king appoint commissioners in every province of his realm to bring all these beautiful girls into the harem at the citadel of Susa. Let them be placed under the care of Hegai, the king's eunuch, who is in charge of the women; and let beauty treatments be given to them. Then let the girl who pleases the king be queen instead of Vashti" (Esther 2:2-4, NIV).

Three criteria would guide the wife-search contest: beauty, youth, and virginity. The words alone would lure any red-blooded male. The counselors knew how to work the king. Further tantalizing him by the repetition of the words "beautiful young virgins," the servants assure the king that every single one of those beautiful young virgins in all of the 127 provinces of the kingdom would be gathered. None would be missed. "Hey, king, you'll be able to choose the best of the best."

We need to note that our modern beauty pageants—Miss Blossomland, Miss Michigan, Miss America, or Miss Universe—are a far cry from the one these guys were suggesting. King Ahasuerus would be the sole judge and jury. His pageant required all contestants to do all that they could to satisfy the sexual desires of the judge (verses 4, 12-14). Each young woman would spend a sexually active night with the king (verse 14). She would have a year in which to polish every seductive art and enhance her beauty by pampering her body and applying the art of costume and cosmetics. During that time she would have to psych herself up for the moment she would pass from the harem of virgins to the king's bedchamber. Ultimately, it would be elegance, charm, physical beauty, and erotic seduction that would carry the day. Scripture says it succinctly: "In the evening she would go in and in the morning she would return to the second harem" (verse 14). She would move from Hegai's harem of virgins to Shaashgaz's harem of concubines.

Obviously the more the young women pleased the king sexually, the higher their scores would be and the greater their chance would be to be called back for another round of judging. "She would not again go in to the king unless the king delighted in her and she was summoned by name" (verse 14). You can be sure they weren't spending that year developing character. For the ultimate prize in this pageant—it would have no runners-up—was the right to marry the king and to be crowned queen. It isn't the way most of us have heard the story.

The image of personally judging all those ravishing young virgins quickly dashed any more thought of Vashti. The lonely king looked for external beauty and interesting sex to fill his inner void.

Tragically, Ahasuerus regretted what he had done to Vashti. He missed and still loved her. It was his foolish drunkenness and male chauvinism that had lost her. Now he was all alone. But rather than admit his mistake, rather than make it right, he allowed himself to take an easier, more face-saving pleasant route—he would just start a new relationship. How often we find ourselves doing the very same thing. Ahasuerus reminds us a lot about our human heart. We can be filled with loneliness and regrets for things we have done. But rather than dealing responsibly with them, too often we'll just go on with life.

Love at First Night

So the search was on, and an obscure young woman named Esther got caught up in the beauty pageant's net. Scripture simply tells us that she was orphaned and had grown up to become a young woman of remarkable beauty. Esther was beautiful in form and lovely to look at, the biblical writer tells us (verse 7). Like every other beauty contestant, she spent her year doing everything needed to make herself physically attractive and alluring to the lonely king. But she had more than that to offer. From the moment Esther hit the harem she stood apart from the crowd. "Esther was taken to the king's palace into the custody of Hegai, who was in charge of the women. Now the young lady pleased him and found favor with him. So he quickly provided her with her cosmetics and food, gave her seven choice maids from the king's palace, and transferred her and her maids to the best place in the harem" (verses 8, 9). Hegai wasn't the only one Esther impressed. She "found favor in the eyes of all who saw her" (verse 15).

Evidently she had a winsomeness, a charming personality, a natural grace befitting a queen.[6] The girl had a way about her that drew one to her. Esther was beautiful not just because she was good-looking. She apparently acted like a queen. Her deportment was queenly.[7] It gave her an advantage over the other women and finally impressed Ahasuerus enough to move him to accept her as his new queen.

Remember, in his heart of hearts Ahasuerus was lonely. He was searching for a companion, a queen—not just an exciting bed partner, although that was part of the pageant. The Persian monarch evaluated her beauty from a wide range of perspectives: her physical appearance as well as her style, her personality, and her demeanor.

Once Ahasuerus met Esther he became enthralled with her. "And the king loved Esther more than all the women, and she found favor and kindness with him more than all the virgins, so that he set the royal crown on her head and made her queen instead of Vashti" (verse 17).

It was love at first night. He not only found pleasure in the evening he spent with her, but he enjoyed her. She struck a chord of honest admiration in his lonely heart. Verse 17 tells us that she found both grace and lovingkindness with the king. Grace *(hēn)* conveys the idea of an elegance, or charm, i.e., a winsome attractiveness. Lovingkindness *(hesed)* suggests a relationship that one has toward another person. It points to a relationship that expresses itself in loyalty, kindness, affection, or mercy toward that person. In other words, Ahasuerus's heart was so drawn out to Esther that he loved her more than any other. No longer lonely, he crowned her queen and threw another party (verse 18). It was a great celebration of love. The king declared a holiday, and everyone was happy.

I want to linger for just a moment on the matter of Esther's character. "At the height of competition, surrounded by sensual, greedy, superficial women, Esther stood alone."[8] In a setting in which women had available to them all the jewelry, all the perfume, all the cosmetics, all the clothing they needed to make them physically attractive and alluring to the lonely king, Esther "was modest about her own person, and she was authentic."[9] "Now when the turn of Esther, the daughter of Abihail the uncle of Mordecai who had taken her as his daughter, came to go in to the king, she did not request anything except what Hegai, the king's eunuch who was in charge of the women, advised" (verse 15).

The passage gives us no sense of what Esther took with her or what she wore or how she smelled when her turn came to spend a night with the king. It simply tells us that she asked for Hegai's advice. Hegai had seen hundreds of women come and go and knew the king's tastes—what turned him on. Esther may have been the most modestly dressed or the most spectacularly adorned. Scripture doesn't say. We know nothing of either Hegai's or the king's tastes in these matters. What we do see here, though, is Esther showing herself to be humble and cooperative. She's not too proud to listen to the wisdom of others. More important, she's not about to put her confidence in artificial beauty aids.[10] Everything Scripture records of Esther's interpersonal relations reveals a truly remarkable young woman whose real beauty was inside.

Weaving a Tangled Web

Every day the Washington *Post* offers a solution to the loneliness many people feel. "Your relationship begins with an ad in PersonalsPlus!" it promises. As you read through the ads, you can laugh at what people either say about themselves or the kind of person they're searching for. Or you can be saddened with the image of lonely people reaching out for love. Listen:

"**A GENUINE** nice Guy. Attractive, athletic, well established SWM [single White male], 39, 5'10", 180#, enjoys power boats, skiing, biking, weekend getaways, no bars/games, ISO [in search of] attractive, reasonably fit, affectionate Woman, under 36, who is ready for a lasting relationship with a Man of great sensitivity and depth."

"**TRIM, FIT** SWF [single White female], 36, attractive, petite, fun, sincere, smart, tender, outgoing, successful F seeking same in S/D/WiM [single, divorced, widowed male], 39-46, 'cowboy' (especially military officer) who does occasional black-tie, but also sports, camping, lots of laughter. RSVP and surprise yourself. God knows this ad's a shock to me."

Quite often you'll read one that says "ISO [someone who] is honest, has no kids, has no hang-ups." This one says it the clearest:

"AFFLUENT, SUCCESSFUL, secure DWPM [divorced White professional male], 50, trim, slim, very athletic. Likes beaches, boating, RVing, dogs, country western music. ISO young S/DWPF [single, divorced White professional female], with postgrad work, very strong-minded, independent. Worked hard and wants to play hard. Please, no baggage; wishes to travel."

"Please, no baggage!" That's pretty blunt if you ask me. Don't bring me your leftover emotional pain, any history that will place a burden on our relationship. Please, no skeletons in the closet that will surprise, no secrets that you hold. I don't want to have to deal with any imperfections or idiosyncrasies in your life. "Please, no baggage."

Good luck! That's a tough one to fill in our broken world.

I'm not sure what all Ahasuerus saw in Esther, but when he set the royal crown on her pretty young head and made her queen instead of Vashti, he had no idea he was crowning a "pretender." He had no idea that this gorgeous young woman of grace and dignity whom he had so madly fallen in love with was carrying some baggage, hiding a secret that would forever change his life and his kingdom.

In the midst of the most gala event the Persian realm perhaps had ever known—this marriage made in Susa, this celebration of love— lurked a deep, dark secret. The author of Esther consciously sets it up for us to see. He wants to shake our sensibilities. "Now the king was attracted to Esther more than to any other of the women, and she won his favor and approval more than any of the other virgins. So he set a royal crown on her head and made her queen instead of Vashti. And the king gave a great banquet, Esther's banquet, for all his nobles and officials. He proclaimed a holiday throughout the provinces and distributed gifts with royal liberality. . . . *But Esther had kept secret her family background and nationality just as Mordecai had told her to do*" (verses 17-20, NIV).

46

Twice the biblical writer tells us that Esther hid her background (and hence her faith) (verses 10, 20). Earlier in the story the narrative declares that "Esther did not make known her people or her kindred, for Mordecai had instructed her that she should not make them known" (verse 10). The flow of events in the story almost seem to say: "There is time for applause and time for pause."[11] In verse 17 we have a Jew elevated. Great! But in verse 20 we have faith that is evaded. Not so good! Esther hides her identity. In the process she buries her faith.

And it is intentional! As such, Esther is a "pretender," an impersonator. What you see is not what you get. *Behind the seen*, she's not what she's all made up to be. Esther seeks to be someone she's not. She doesn't show who she really is.

What's going on here? Is it simply a matter of "being wise as a serpent and harmless as a dove"? The point, I think, appears in that very first reference to Esther in verses 5-7 of chapter 2. There we confront a surprise—"Now there was a Jew in Susa the capital whose name was Mordecai" (verse 5). Mordecai was Esther's cousin, her foster father (verse 7). More important, his ancestors were from Jerusalem. They "had been taken into exile from Jerusalem with the captives who had been exiled with Jeconiah king of Judah, whom Nebuchadnezzar the king of Babylon had exiled" (verse 6). In other words, Mordecai's ancestors were part of that first wave of Hebrew captives rounded up by Babylon's King Nebuchadnezzar that we read about in 2 Kings 24:1-16. What makes this particular detail so startling for this story is that Cyrus the Great, a previous Medo-Persian king, had declared some 50 years earlier that the Jews could return to their homeland. A second decree by Darius then followed. Yet this Jew, Mordecai—whose ancestors came from Jerusalem—is living not only in exile but at the very heart of the pagan kingdom—in Susa, Persia's capital city.[12]

Is it becoming clearer? A Jew from Jerusalem is living in Susa—someone who should be in the capital of God's sphere of influence instead dwells in the capital of the world's sphere of influence. Someone who should be minding God's ways gets caught up in the world's. And so we confront the reality of God's people yielding to worldly pressures. Obviously many of the exiles had no "next year in Jerusalem" kind of feeling.

The narrator's point is that both Mordecai and Esther "have their sights set on earthly affairs and not spiritual matters." [13] They typify the average Jewish man and woman of the Exile. Barry Davis says it well when he observes that for the most part, God's people "had adopted the customs and social conventions of the surrounding heathen nation. They blended in with their pagan neighbors to such an extent that, at least in the case of Mordecai and Esther, distinguishing them from their secular neighbors was virtually impossible." [14] You cannot avoid that conclusion when you read the text carefully.

Esther, then, presents the paradox of a good person. She was winsome, lovely to be around, a person of unselfish modesty and authenticity. And yet she was someone caught up with the things of the world at the expense of her faith and her relationship with God. You didn't really know where she stood with God.

"Now, wait a minute," you protest. "Esther was forced into this. She got caught in the great beauty-pageant net and found herself swept along against her will. And it was Mordecai's idea for her to keep quiet about her faith. She was just being obedient. Trying to please her foster father."

Were the women forced to participate in the competition? Interestingly, the story doesn't say one way or another. If they weren't compelled, Esther's faith would be incriminated for sure. But if the women had no choice, we still have the question of her evasion of faith. Why does neither Esther nor Mordecai offer any protest to the process by which Esther at best would be married to a pagan, and at worst live for the rest of her life as a concubine in the king's harem? What would have happened if she had disclosed her faith? Would the authorities have disqualified her from the start, or would she have found herself living as a concubine anyway the rest of her life? Was playing up to the king and keeping her faith private the only way to avoid a "living death"—that is, life in the harem? Why didn't she take a stand, as Daniel did? Maybe it had something to do with her being a woman in a man's world? I think not!

We'll never know in this life the answers to such questions. But we can be certain that if Mordecai and Esther had been in Jerusalem, where God wanted them to be, they wouldn't have found themselves in their predicament now. Furthermore, had they revealed their faith, stood up for what was right, the story of Esther, for sure, would be a very different one, to say the least. Had Haman known the true Esther, he likely would not have hatched his diabolical scheme of genocide. More important, "God then would have been able to work through the faithfulness of His people rather than despite their unfaithfulness."[15]

So a lonely world gets pretending people! That's Esther. A world may admire us but not find God or truth readily apparent (or anywhere, for that matter) in our lives. It's ironic—a broken world, a house of cards, searching for meaning to fill the God-shaped void in its heart, often finds God's own people pretending to be (or wanting to be) just like them!

Human Odds and God's Ends

Mount Si in North Bend, Washington, is an absolutely impressive sight. That's why it was the film location for the provocative television series *Twin Peaks*. The first time I saw Mount Si was an unexaggerated surprise. I didn't even know it was there. I was driving up from Seattle to Snoqualmie Pass just to hang around and see the mountains and get a feel for some really deep snow (higher than many buildings). But it was an overcast day. Snowing here and there. And the views of the mountains weren't that good. Hungry, I pulled into North Bend to find something to eat. Spotting a quaint little pizza shop that claimed to make great Chicago-style pizza, I stepped in and was soon eating great pizza and sipping local brewed root beer. My table sat right next to a large floor-to-ceiling window that promised views out the back of the building. All I could see, though, was low-hanging fog, so I busied myself with food. One of the times I looked up from my plate, the clouds were gone, and Mount Si stared me in the face. It was an in-your-face kind of thing. Dropping my fork, I gazed at the sight. I had no idea this kind of mountain was hiding right there behind the fog.

When we read a chapter like this one, all we seem to see is a lonely king and a pretending queen—Mr. Lonely and the Pretender. But if the fog of human brokenheartedness and quiet compromise lifted, we'd catch a magnificent view of God.

We'd find a God who can beat the odds. If Las Vegas oddsmakers existed in the days of Esther, what odds would they have given that an orphaned Jewish girl living in exile would one day sit on the throne as queen? One in a hundred? One in a thousand? One in a million? Few, if any, would have predicted she'd be the winner, the new Miss Persia. But despite the odds and because of the grace of God, Esther became the empire's queen.

If the fog would lift and we could get a clear view of our awesome *behind the seen* God, we would find a God active even in the midst of our compromises. In the last chapter we learned that God works among the carnal and secular decisions of our house-of-cards world. Here we learn that God continues His plans even when His own people compromise and hide their identity. Even when they don't love Him first and last and best. In an incredible and unimaginable way God can take our often poor choices and make them fit into His bigger picture of sovereign grace. Isn't that a wonderful picture of God?

God desires our good. He knows our real need. While He will never force Himself upon us, He will always be *behind the seen* working in our behalf. When faith is private, character and identity are at risk, but God is still at work to strengthen our character and to remind us who we really are. That's the direction the book of Esther takes us.

In his poem *Marmion* Sir Walter Scott laments: "Oh, what a tangled web we weave, when first we practice to deceive!" Marmion eventually regretted the deceptive events that he had set in motion. How could he even stop the consequences of those events?

Only God can untangle the web of compromise we weave. God does not condone our compromises. Sometimes, as in the case of Esther, He does not even make explicit judgment on them. He may not even clarify exactly what those compromises might be. The book of Esther leaves much to our imagination. A lot of things that we read in Esther we just cannot explain. But each one of us has to read the passage in a way that confronts us with the reality of our own compromises. It forces us to search between the lines, always asking our-selves what "our" compromises might be. Obviously, they are differ-ent for each one of us and often distinct for each generation. The important thing is what God does with our compromises. As Gerald Wheeler writes: "Throughout the book of Esther we find things that we do not understand. . . . Such things happened, and the important thing to the biblical writer was what God did with them. God's spokes-men wanted to show how He could bring good out of any situation, no matter how tangled or seemingly hopeless it might be."[16]

Mr. Lonely and the Pretender. *Behind the seen* is the lonely heart of a rich and powerful king. *Behind the seen* is the hidden (or languid) faith of a beautiful young woman. And *behind the seen* is the sovereign hand of a caring, compassionate, and loving God working for you and me.

Fortunately God does not pretend. He simply engages us in the set-ting of the decisions we make, whether faithful or compromising.

Let me raise a question just now. Are you a Jew living in Susa? Are you living in the sphere of this world's influence when God would have you in the sphere of His influence? Are you busy with the busi-ness of this world when God would have you involved with His busi-ness? If so, I pray that God will lift the fog so you will see Mount Si staring you in the face. That you'll see a wonderful God who alone is worthy of our trust and love.

---

[1] Richard E. Byrd, *Alone* (New York: G. P. Putnam's Sons, 1938); Richard E. Byrd, "Alone," *Reader's Digest Condensed Books* (Pleasantville, N.Y.: Reader's Digest Association, 1964), vol. 2, pp. 301-356.
[2] A. B. Luter and B. C. Davis, *God Behind the Seen*, p. 145, n. 5.
[3] *Ibid.*, p. 145.
[4] J. D. Levenson, *Esther*, p. 54.
[5] C. R. Swindoll, *Esther: A Woman of Strength and Dignity*, p. 34.
[6] A. M. Rodríguez, *Esther: A Theological Approach*, p. 67.
[7] *Ibid.*, p. 68.
[8] Swindoll, p. 52.
[9] *Ibid.*, p. 49.
[10] Rodríguez, p. 68.
[11] Luter and Davis, p. 168.
[12] *Ibid.*, pp. 148, 149.
[13] *Ibid.*, p. 159.
[14] *Ibid.*, p. 179.
[15] *Ibid.*, p. 157.
[16] Gerald Wheeler, *Footprints of God* (Boise, Idaho: Pacific Press Pub. Assn., 1987), p. 86.

CHAPTER FOUR

IF YOU UNDERSTAND THIS, YOU'RE IN TROUBLE

Esther 2:21-3:6

Back when the telegraph was the fastest method of long-distance communication, a young man applied for a job as a Morse code operator. Answering an ad in the newspaper, he went to the office address listed. When he arrived, he entered a large, busy office filled with noise and clatter, including the sound of the telegraph in the background. A sign on the receptionist's counter instructed job applicants to fill out a form and wait until someone took them to enter the inner office.

Taking a form, the young man filled it out and sat down with the seven other applicants in the waiting area. After a few minutes he stood up, crossed the room to the door of the inner office, and walked right in. Naturally the other applicants perked up, wondering what was going on. Muttering among themselves that they hadn't heard any summons yet, they assumed that the applicant who went into the office made a mistake and would be disqualified. Within a few minutes, however, the employer escorted the young man out of the office and said to the other applicants, "Gentlemen, thank you very much for coming, but the job has just been filled."

The other applicants began grumbling to one another, and one protested, "Wait a minute. I don't understand. He was the last to come in, and we never even got a chance to be interviewed. Yet he got the job. That's not fair!"

"I'm sorry," the employer said, "but all the time you've been sitting here, the telegraph has been ticking out the following message in Morse code: 'If you understand this message, then come right in. The job is yours.' None of you heard it or understood it. This young man did. The job is his."

Mordecai had been sitting at the king's gate for nearly four years when the king promoted Haman above all the Medo-Persian princes who advised the king.[1] "After these events King Ahasuerus promoted Haman, the son of Hammedatha the Agagite, and advanced him and established his authority over all the princes who *were* with him" (Esther 3:1). Since he's not listed among the seven princes during Ahasuerus's third year (Esther 1:14), Haman must have ascended to the position of prime minister rather quickly.[2] His sudden rise to power caught Mordecai by surprise, making him sit up and take note. It registered a very subtle but clear message in his mind. Mordecai heard a voice from God—the divine rhythm of Morse code ticking in the background against the clatter of a Persian world in which people were distracted with life and unable to hear. The voice from God declared, "If you understand this . . . you're in pretty big trouble! It's time to take a stand."

Staring Evil in the Face

Morse code is a system of dots, dashes, and pauses once used to send all radio and telegraph messages. The dot results from quickly pressing and releasing the key of the telegraph sender. It produces a rapid *click-clack* sound in the receiver at the other end. The operator makes a dash by holding down the key longer, thus prolonging the time between the *click* and the *clack*. Spaces are pauses between *click-clacks* of dots and dashes. Particular sequences and durations of *click-clacks* represent the letters of the alphabet. A is a dot and a dash, B a dash and three dots, and so on. The rhythm of *click-clack* ticks along at a fairly rapid pace. If you know the code and your ear can catch the rhythm of *click-clacks*, you can decipher the message. That is, if you're listening.

A few dots and dashes can easily get lost in the *click-clack* rhythm of this story. If Mordecai had missed them, he would have been doomed. And if you and I miss them, we'll not only misunderstand the story of Esther, we could be doomed as well. What are those dots and dashes? What was the code ticking out its message in Mordecai's mind? Haman was an Agagite (Esther 3:1). That may sound like some kind of rock you can find on a rock hunt out West, but Mordecai knew exactly what that meant. And it sent chills up his spine.

I want to stop for a moment and point out a very clear, but not always obvious, contrast that the book of Esther creates between Mordecai and Haman. Something Mordecai understood immediately may not be all that important to us at first glance. Earlier in the narrative it tells us "there was a Jew in Susa the capital whose name was Mordecai, the son of Jair, the son of Shimei, the son of Kish, a Benjamite" (Esther 2:5). Here we learn that Haman is "the son of Hammedatha the Agagite" (Esther 3:1). "So what?" you say. Well, the point of Mordecai's lineage is to show some connection, direct or indirect, to King Saul, who also was a son of Kish, a Benjamite. And Haman's lineage connects him in some way with the Amalekite king Agag. No other characters in the book of Esther have anything said about their lineage, including Ahasuerus, although mentioned 167 times.

If you know your biblical history, you will remember that the Amalekites were the ones who mercilessly and ruthlessly attacked the Israelites who lagged behind in their march from Egypt to Canaan (Deut. 25:17, 18; Ex. 17:8-16). The Amalekites were an idolatrous people who had no respect whatsoever for Israel's God (Deut. 25:18). They proved to be lifelong bitter enemies of the Jews. The day came when God instructed Saul to eradicate the Amalekites once and for all. They had filled up their cup of rebellion against God and animosity toward His people. While Saul defeated the Amalekite king, he did not kill him (1 Sam. 15). "The Agagites, descendants of the Amalekites, got their name from the king that Saul didn't kill."[3]

In short, a long-standing family feud had been going on here, reaching back more than 900 years before the events recorded in the book of Esther take place.[4] Like the ethnic and religious rivalries in Ireland, the Middle East, Rwanda, Yugoslavia, or Kosovo, where the resentments between age-old enemies sometimes pass down through succeeding generations. It undoubtedly was the case with Haman. He, too, nurtured incredible hatred toward the Jews. His hatred was like a time bomb waiting to explode. Mordecai simply provided Haman with the opportunity to awaken his dormant hatred.[5] That's why Haman's full name later includes the contemptuous label "the enemy of the Jews" (Esther 3:10). Haman literally incarnated the original hostility, the original hatred, and the absolutely brutal evil of his forefathers.[6] He personified evil.

"OK," you say, "what's the point?"

When the Persian king promoted Haman to prime minister, Mordecai suddenly understood something extremely important about his contemporary world. He was a Jew from Jerusalem living in Susa (Esther 2:5, 6), caught up with the business of his Persian world rather than God's business. Someone who should have been in the capital of God's sphere of influence rather than in the capital of the world's sphere of influence. But life in Persia had gotten pretty good. In fact, life in Persia could not have been much better. Esther was queen. He, an official at the king's gate, had even saved the king's life. Humanly speaking, Mordecai and his people were as secure as any exiled people could possibly be.[7] They, along with their Persian neighbors, were enjoying the good life.

When Mordecai saw Haman now at Persia's helm as prime minister, the principal shaker and the mover behind the king, he realized that things in his comfortable little world were not as benign, not as harmless, not as safe, not as innocent as he first thought. Suddenly the awesome Persian Empire—with all its magnificent human achievements, with all its splendor and the good life it both provided and promised—held tremendous capacity for evil. He realized it was inherently anti-God and naturally in opposition to His people.[8] Mordecai knew he was staring evil in the face—evil that would ultimately destroy him. It was a wake-up call.

One cannot help wondering if it took the promotion of Haman to Persia's prime minister to shake Mordecai out of his comfortable slumber. Could it be that nothing else would have broken Persia's bewitching hold on him and his people? Could it be that the God who "changes the times and the epochs; . . . [and who] removes kings and establishes kings" (Dan. 2:21) knew that Mordecai would understand that he was encountering evil only if he saw in it the face of the likes of Haman, an Agagite? I think so. The God who had Esther waiting in the wings to fill the vacancy left by Vashti was the same God who allowed Haman's rapid rise to the pinnacle of power. No doubt Satan was working too. *Prophets and Kings* tells us that "Satan himself, the hidden instigator of the scheme, was trying to rid the earth of those who preserved the knowledge of the true God."[9] But God knew that not just any old ruthless anti-Semitic prime minister would do. It would take an Agagite—someone like Haman—to do the trick. There needed to be some kind of unmistakable code that would unleash its pregnant imagery in Mordecai's imagination if he was to catch what was really going on in his world before it was too late.

Mordecai and his people were like the proverbial frog in the kettle. Completely unaware of the danger they were in, they could not discern the quiet shift in temperature that would soon cook them for eternity. That's why God chose something radical—an unmistakable code whose meaning could not be missed. An Agagite ascending to prime minister was the way to catch Mordecai's attention. It is part of the surprise and irony of this little book that God uses the very thing that will destroy them to awaken spiritual passion among His people and accomplish His purposes for them.

Hey, I'm a Jew

Providentially, Mordecai caught the subtle message God relayed when "all the king's servants who were at the king's gate bowed down and paid homage to Haman; for so the king had commanded concerning him. . . . Mordecai neither bowed down nor paid homage" (Esther 3:2).

"Wait a minute," you say. "It wouldn't matter who Ahasuerus made prime minister, Mordecai still wouldn't have bowed down."

Well, I'm not so sure about that. Let's look closer.

Mordecai's response was no quick "Jews don't bow down to officials because of the second commandment" kind of stuff. The simple honoring of an officer would present no problems for a cosmopolitan Jew such as Mordecai, who had taught his foster daughter humility and respect, allowed her to marry a Gentile king, and then counseled her repeatedly for nearly five years to keep quiet about her faith. "Don't let anybody know who you really are or what you believe," he repeatedly advised.[10]

Furthermore, it was quite common for Jews and other peoples of the East to bow to those in high office or those whom they respected.

Abraham bowed to the Canaanite sons of Heth (Gen. 23:7). Jacob bowed to Esau (Gen. 33:3). Jacob's sons bowed to Joseph, the governor of Egypt (Gen. 42:6). We find David bowing to Saul (1 Sam. 24:8), the woman of Tekoa bowing to David (2 Sam. 14:4), and Bathsheba to David (1 Kings 1:16). Even Esther prostrates herself before King Ahasuerus (Esther 8:3).

Besides, Mordecai had hidden his own faith quite well. He had simply asked Esther to do what he himself was doing. Look at the reaction of his colleagues at the king's gate when they noticed he wasn't bowing to Haman: "Then the king's servants who were at the king's gate said to Mordecai, 'Why are you transgressing the king's command?'" (Esther 3:3). It was obviously something new that they hadn't seen in Mordecai before. The text further suggests that the colleagues at the king's gate were apparently Mordecai's friends, or at least good acquaintances or working buddies, because when they discovered that he was acting in disobedience to the king's command, they didn't immediately report him. Their first reaction was to question him about his actions (verses 3, 4). Every day they asked him about his unusual and uncustomary behavior (verse 4). No doubt, because they liked him and were friends, his fellow servants kept encouraging him to comply with the king's command. At bottom, though, they were trying to understand. It tells us that Mordecai's colleagues at the king's gate really didn't know that much about Mordecai's private life. They certainly didn't have a clear picture of what it meant to be a Jew.

Obviously, in a cosmopolitan setting such as Susa, diversity in racial and religious things kind of blurred or seemed unimportant. Like our modern world, we don't often notice what others around us do or don't do. We work alongside people every day, carpool perhaps, play on the same soccer team, have kids in the same grade at school, but never really get to know each other or reveal that much about ourselves. Many in our world don't know whether we are Christians or not. How easily we keep quiet about our Adventist heritage. Mordecai was not that much different. The fact is, he had done a pretty good job of keeping his faith private. Now, however, in that single act of refusing to bow to Haman (Esther 3:2), he could no longer hide his identity. Even then,

Haman did not notice Mordecai. Someone had to tell him. Only when Mordecai's colleagues point him out does Haman stop to look for himself (verses 4, 5). "Yeah, this is just like a Jew! I had no idea we had one this close to the king." Then, as if by selective perception, Haman sees Mordecai everywhere and becomes consumed with getting even.

Something deeper is going on here than the mere honoring or ignoring of officials in public office. It is something more than a mere "Jews don't bow down to officials because of the second commandment" kind of thing. When Mordecai saw Haman at the top of Persia's political ladder he realized that he could no longer play spiritual games or be lukewarm. He could no longer go for all the gusto his Persian world had to offer, because, at bottom, it all had to do with worship—the loyalty of his heart either to God or to the world. Haman simply personified what was really at stake. Somehow, bowing down and paying homage to Haman went beyond an individual, beyond simple courtesy and respect for a man in high office. It extended to veneration, to where his heart had focused its affections. Perhaps that's why the Hebrew words used here—$k\bar{a}ra'$ ("to bow down") and $\check{s}\bar{a}h\bar{a}(h)$ ("to prostrate oneself")—occur in connection with the worship of either the true God or false gods.[11] The expressions give us a clue toward the deeper issue at stake. They portray the undeniable fact "that Haman's desire was not that men bow in respect for his office and authority, but that they bow and pay homage to Haman as deity (3:5)."[12] That appears to be the case as Haman later takes upon himself the power of life, death, and judgment in a great ethnic purge.[13] Haman symbolized everything Mordecai had been grasping for in Persian culture. Suddenly he realized it had become a matter of life or death. In reality it always had been. But now Mordecai saw it clearly.

As these things dawned upon him, Mordecai recognized that he had to do something radical. "If you understand this," he heard God's message tell him, "you're in pretty big trouble. It's time to take a stand." How long before he decided we'll never know, but as Haman strutted by the king's gate and "all the king's servants who were at the king's gate bowed down and paid homage to Haman" "Mordecai neither bowed down nor paid homage" (verse 2).

From that moment on Mordecai could no longer hide his identity. "He had told them that he was a Jew" (verse 4). Note the spiritual principle that when we defy evil we own our identity. When we take a stand for God we accept and are in control of who we are. Up till now, Mordecai had commanded Esther to disguise her identity as a Jew. Not surprisingly, Mordecai was first to disclose his identity, and when he did, it triggered an all-out attempt to destroy both him and his people.[14] Now we get a closer look at evil's real nature. We see revealed seething anger, deceitful manipulations, distorted truth, bold-faced lies, bribes, false accusations, and finally, a death warrant. The die are rolled and the full measure of evil unfurls to destroy those who would follow God (see verses 5-15).

This brings us back to a theme expressed first in Vashti's moral choice—when you disobey the king, when you reject the will of our world (and the Hamans of this world), when you stand for what is right, history will never be the same.[15] Every time someone in the book of Esther resists the world's power, chooses to do the right thing, the course of history alters and God works in surprising ways. Reversals take place, and people change. But although the world is different, it may well exact a price from those who take a personal stand for what is morally right.[16] Yet such obedience sets God free to do things He might otherwise not be able do for His people or the lost individuals of our world.

Oswald Chambers puts the obedience/history link this way: "We are so involved in the universal purposes of God that immediately we obey God, others are affected. . . . We can disobey God if we choose, and it will bring immediate relief to the situation, but we shall be a grief to our Lord. Whereas if we obey God, He will look after those who have been pressed into the consequences of our obedience. We have simply to obey and to leave all consequences with Him."[17] Chambers further asserts that "if we obey God it is going to cost other people more than it costs us, and that is where the sting comes in. If we are in love with our Lord, obedience does not cost us anything, it is a delight, but it costs those who do not love Him a good deal. If we obey God it will mean that other people's plans are upset, and they will gibe us with it—'You call this Christianity?' "[18] Mordecai soon learned the principle well. Not only did his obedience to God put his people under threat of death; it threw the entire city of Susa into confusion (verse 15). The next few months were a frightening threat of holocaust.

Symbolic Beginning

In the prologue to his biography on Alexander Solzhenitsyn, D. M. Thomas tells of asking a retired KGB colonel what image he would choose to represent the beginning of Russia's frightening Bolshevik era. For a long time the old colonel gazed out the window. "I would choose," he replied at last, "a moment described in Nathan Milstein's autobiography. As a *symbolic* beginning, you understand. Milstein was a music student in Petersburg during World War I. And he writes that in 1916, in the winter, he was walking along the Moika Canal. In front of the Yousoupov Palace he heard agitated voices, and saw people craning to look over the parapet into the frozen river. So Milstein looked down too, and saw that some of the ice was broken, and there, the water had pink swirls in it. People around him were shouting, 'Rasputin! Bastard! Serves him right!' Milstein realized the pinkish swirls were the blood of Rasputin—one of the most powerful men in the empire. Imagine it: hurrying along a frozen canal—a day in December like this one, perhaps late for a violin lesson—and you see Rasputin's blood! . . . Well, I've seen lots of blood, even shed quite a lot of it. . . . But anyway, if I were a writer, or maybe a filmmaker, that's how I'd start: looking down at broken ice and seeing swirls of blood. Like a dream . . ."[19]

What image would you choose to represent the agelong controversy between Satan and God's people? What image would you select to typify the frightening issues God's people will face once more in the end-time?

Could it be the story of Esther? "Could Mordecai as a descendant of Saul and Haman as a descendant of Agag be archetypes of a renewed battle against the archenemy of God's people?"[20] Could it be that "as Haman stands against all who represent the true God, the final Man of

Sin, the Antichrist, will stand in opposition to all that Jesus Christ represents"?[21] I think so.

Remember, Esther has a future orientation,[22] an eschatological aspect to its message. In effect, the story of Esther is typological.[23] God intended that these things be written for our example (1 Cor. 10:11; Rom. 15:4). The deadly encounter with evil in Esther points to a future in which the face of Haman will one day appear again. *Prophets and Kings* tells us that in the last days "Satan will arouse indignation against the minority who refuse to accept popular customs and traditions."[24] The Apocalypse of John tells of a time when those who refuse to worship the beast will be under threat of death. "And there was given to him to give breath to the image of the beast, that the image of the beast might even speak and cause as many as do not worship the image of the beast to be killed. And he causes all, the small and the great, and the rich and the poor, and the free men and the slaves, to be given a mark on their right hand, or on their forehead, and *he provides* that no one should be able to buy or to sell, except the one who has the mark, *either* the name of the beast or the number of his name" (Rev. 13:15-17).

The KGB officer's vision of pinkish swirls of blood on broken ice is apt imagery of how Revelation paints the final showdown. In that day the words of Haman to King Ahasuerus will be spoken again: "There is a certain people scattered and dispersed among the peoples in all the provinces of your kingdom; their laws are different from those of all other people, and they do not observe the king's laws, so it is not in the king's interest to let them remain" (Esther 3:8). The trying experience of Esther will repeat itself on a global scale, reaching down to that hour in which the dragon is angry and launches war with the woman and the remnant of her seed, those who keep the commandments of God and have Jesus' testimony (Rev. 12:17).

Again, the words of Ellen White poignantly link the two pivotal moments of Esther's day and the last days. "The trying experiences that came to God's people in the days of Esther were not peculiar to that age alone. The revelator, looking down the ages to the close of time, has declared, 'The dragon was wroth with the woman, and went to make war with the remnant of her seed, which keep the commandments of God, and have the testimony of Jesus Christ' (Rev. 12:17). . . . The decree that will finally go forth against the remnant people of God will be very similar to that issued by Ahasuerus against the Jews. Today the enemies of the true church see in the little company keeping the Sabbath commandment a Mordecai at the gate. The reverence of God's people for His law is a constant rebuke to those who have cast off the fear of the Lord and are trampling on His Sabbath. . . . Today, as in the days of Esther and Mordecai, the Lord will vindicate His truth and His people." [25]

"The Protestant world today sees in the little company keeping the Sabbath a Mordecai in the gate. His character and conduct, expressing reverence for the law of God, are a constant rebuke to those who have cast off the fear of the Lord and are trampling upon His Sabbath; the unwelcome intruder must by some means be put out of the way." [26]

Eight job applicants. Each sitting in a busy noise-filled office. Each waiting for an interview for a job as a Morse code operator. All the while they wait, a telegraph has been ticking in the background noise of a busy office the announcement in Morse code: "If you understand this message, then come right in. The job is yours."

Only one stopped to hear the *click-clack* rhythm of the receiver and understood its coded message. Because of it, he alone stood up and walked through the door and got the job.

We live in a world that's full of business and clatter, much like that office. As the case of God's people in Esther's day, the noise of all that our world has to offer distracts us. We are unable to hear the still small voice of God as He speaks through the signs of our times or even the events taking place in our own everyday lives. So often we're not thinking about what's taking place around us. We don't stop to consider the moral/spiritual implications of our own personal decisions or even where our world is headed.

Esther sets forth an awesome picture of a loving God who sends His people messages of warning. A God who does not allow us to continue on in our slumber or our compromise but is working *behind the seen* to awaken us to what looms on the horizon. His warnings are usually in some subtle but understandable code. He designs a warning message for each one of us. It can be some sign in our world or personal life—something we read, see, or experience. Whatever it is, God says, "If you understand this, you're in pretty big trouble. It's time to take a stand."

God is our friend who will not let us drift alone without a warning in a dangerous hell-bound world. Compromise may suck the moral and spiritual discernment out of us, but God is still working to reach us. He gives opportunity for us to understand evil's nature. Mordecai received the message because he caught the code. Again, it is part of the surprise and irony of this little book that God uses the very thing that will destroy them to arouse spiritual passion among His people and accomplish His purposes for them. He will do it again in the end. God will work through His Holy Spirit in a way carefully designed to awaken His lethargic people. Some will miss His work or warning altogether, because they are not watching or waiting. They will not be up on the issues, because they will be unfamiliar with His Word. As a result they will neither understand their identity nor have the opportunity to change the course of history opening before them. Tragically, they will miss the subtle but still understandable code. If they had only watched, prayed, and listened.

Behind the seen of this world lurks a deadly evil with but one passion—to destroy you and me.

Behind the seen of many of God's people is a faith that has grown tired and lukewarm and must be awakened. We have an identity that needs to be openly revealed and claimed.

Behind the seen is a merciful gracious God who relentlessly works His sovereign providence in a way that would help us see the evil staring us in the face. He does not seek to frighten or paralyze us, but to enable us to discover that He is there to empower and preserve us if we but fully own our identity as His daughter, His son, His remnant people.

---

[1] A four-year span occurred between Esther's coronation (Esther 2:16, 17) and Haman's casting lots to find the best day to exterminate the Jews (Esther 3:7).

[2] Jack W. Hayford, ed., *Redemption and Restoration* (Nashville: Thomas Nelson Publishers, 1996), p. 102.

[3] C. R. Swindoll, *Esther: A Woman of Strength and Dignity,* p. 64.

[4] A. B. Luter and B. C. Davis, *God Behind the Seen,* p. 199.

[5] A. M. Rodríguez, *Esther: A Theological Approach,* pp. 58, 59.

[6] *Ibid.,* p. 58.

[7] Luter and Davis, p. 195.

[8] E. H. Merrill, *A Biblical Theology of the Old Testament,* p. 203.

[9] E. G. White, *Prophets and Kings,* p. 601.

[10] Hayford, p. 104.

[11] Luter and Davis, p. 202. "Both terms also occur in a variety of nonreligious settings. Often they depict bowing down in respect of one person to another. The context in which they are found dictates the specifics of how each is to be interpreted" *(ibid.).*

[12] Hayford, p. 108.

[13] *Ibid.*

[14] Merrill, p. 203.

[15] Rodríguez, p. 53.

[16] *Ibid.*

[17] Oswald Chambers, "What My Obedience to God Costs Other People," *My Utmost for His Highest,* reading for January 11.

[18] *Ibid.*

[19] D. M. Thomas, *Alexander Solzhenitsyn: A Century in His Life* (New York: St. Martin's Press, 1998), p. xiii.

[20] Hayford, p. 103.

[21] *Ibid.,* p. 108.

[22] Rodríguez, p. 107.

[23] Biblical typology is based on the principle of repetition and enlargement. A historical event or actual person in a concrete local situation becomes a God-ordained paradigm or illustration illuminating the moral spiritual issues in some larger sphere. In the case of Esther, the actual historical experience of crisis produces theological perspectives that will find universal application in the end time.

[24] White, p. 605.

[25] *Ibid.,* pp. 605, 606.

[26] Ellen G. White, *Testimonies for the Church* (Mountain View, Calif.: Pacific Press Pub. Assn., 1948), vol. 5, p. 450.

CHAPTER FIVE

THIS IS YOUR HOUR, STAND! SPEAK! DIE! JUST DON'T BE SILENT

Esther 4:1-16

The White people of New Orleans were scared. So were the Blacks. A federal judge had ordered the city to open its public schools to Black children, and the parents decided that if they had to let Black children in, they would keep their White children out. They let it be known that any Black children who came to school would be in trouble. So the Black children stayed home too.

Except for Ruby Bridges, that is. Her parents sent her to school all by herself. She was just 6 years old and the first and, for the better part of that 1961 school year, the only Black child to attend class in a White New Orleans school.

Every morning Ruby walked alone through a heckling crowd of protesters to an empty school. White people lined up on both sides of the way and shook their fists at her. Yelling, sneering, holding signs, they threatened to do terrible things to her if she kept coming to their school. But every morning at 10 minutes to 8:00 Ruby walked, head up, eyes ahead, straight through the angry mob. Two U.S. marshals walked ahead of her, and two walked behind her. She then spent the day alone with her teachers inside that big silent school building.

Like others, Harvard University professor Robert Coles was curious about Ruby's courage and went down to find out what made her tick. Why was she able to stand up to such constant pressure day in and day out? Coles talked with Ruby's mother, and in his book *The Moral Life of Children* he tells us what Ruby's mother had to say on the matter: "There's a lot of people who talk about doing good, and a lot of people who argue about what's good and what's not good," but some "just put their lives on the line for what's right."[1] While a lot of people were debating the issues of racially integrated schools or merely talking about doing what was right, 6-year-old Ruby Bridges put her life on the line and did it. She had a bit of grit, something in her heart that transferred to her feet.

Esther had that kind of grit. She, too, came to that moment in life when she put her life on the line for what was right, and something in her heart transferred to her feet: "I will go in to the king," she announced, "which is not according to the law; and if I perish, I perish" (Esther 4:16).

Here is the Esther most of us know—Esther at her best, a woman of courage and grit and a hero of faith.

Before this point in her story, though, she has done some things that we might legitimately wonder about or question. She had apparent compromises in her life that make us nervous, human imperfections that challenge our traditional view of this biblical hero. Up till now, Esther has kept her faith private. Like Mordecai and other lukewarm Jews of the Diaspora, she had been caught up in the good life of Persia. But now a special strength fills her. She puts her life on the line for what's right. "If I perish, I perish," she announces. From that moment on no one can ever again doubt her allegiance to her people or her God.

Why the turnaround? What made the difference? Why was Esther so willing now to unfurl her Jewish colors after five years of careful secrecy?

This Is Your Hour

After nine grueling days of Mideast peace talks at the Wye River Plantation in Maryland, Israel and the Palestinians were back on the road to peace.[2] Israel's security concerns dominated the October 1998 negotiations that drew together such heads of state as Israel's Benjamin Netanyahu, PLO chairman Yasser Arafat, the late Jordan's King Hussein, and United States president Bill Clinton for face-to-face dialogue. Finally, in exchange for more West Bank land, Israel won a detailed Palestinian pledge to conduct a war on terrorism. One of the sticking points was the Palestinian charter that called for the total destruction of Israel. After all, how can two people talk peace if the very national charter of one party in the dialogue demands the complete annihilation of the other? Round and round they went on that one until the Palestinians officially agreed to cut the inflammatory language.

Even as the deal makers were earnestly at work, a Palestinian terrorist lobbed two grenades into a crowded bus station in Beersheba, wounding scores of innocent civilians. On the heels of signing the Wye Accord another Palestinian terrorist driving a carload of explosives attempted to ram a bus carrying 40 Israeli children to school. An Israeli soldier died in the blast he courageously diverted from the bus.

One can only imagine what it's like to be a people marked for death—to have it in official, state-sponsored writing, no less.

The Israeli holocaust museum in Jerusalem has a large bronze statue of a faceless Jewish woman holding a lifeless child in her arms. As you look across the well-manicured lawn and see her, you realize that she portrays the unimaginable anguish, pain, and sorrow the Jewish people have experienced through the generations. It forcefully depicts the reality that there exists a calculating enemy that destroys ruthlessly and thoroughly. How often have Jeremiah's agonizing words rung true for the Jewish people: "A voice is heard in Ramah, lamentation and bitter weeping. Rachel is weeping for her children; she refuses to be comforted for her children, because they are no more" (Jer. 31:15).

Not only did the sinister edict Haman concocted call for the complete destruction of the Jewish people in the Persian Empire; it marked a date on the calendar as well: Adar 13. It was to be one fell swoop. "Then the king's scribes were summoned on the thirteenth day of the first month, and it was written just as Haman commanded. . . . Letters were sent by couriers to all the king's provinces to destroy, to kill, and to annihilate all the Jews, both young and old, women and children, in one day, the thirteenth day of the twelfth month, which is the month of Adar, and to seize their possessions as plunder" (Esther 3:12, 13).

In case you wonder what impact this decree had on the Gentile community, just read the last verse in chapter 3: "The couriers went out impelled by the king's command while the decree was issued in

Susa the capital; and while the king and Haman sat down to drink, the city of Susa was in confusion" (verse 15).

Haman and the king execute a document that calls for the ethnic cleansing of an unwanted people and then sit down for a few beers. It reveals just how disconnected we can sometimes get from the moral reality of our behavior and the disturbing impact such actions have on other people's lives. While Haman and Ahasuerus sat down over their drinks in the palace, the general public wandered around the streets in bewilderment and confusion not unlike those in or near the Jewish ghettos and other European scenes of horror of the late thirties and early forties. "What's going on here?" "Why have those in authority ordered this?" What terror struck their hearts? What fear filled their minds? What moral outrage blazed in them? We see it graphically illustrated in the irony exhibited by Oscar Schindler in his heroic attempts to save 1,000 Jewish workers during the Holocaust. A philandering Gentile prone to the proverbial wine and women, he nevertheless stood aghast at the ethnic cleansing taking place before his very eyes and did something about it. He couldn't just watch it happen. According to the book of Esther, the common man or woman in the street couldn't make sense of it all either.

When a bomb explodes, the blast often affects people even at a distance. The percussion may deafen them or knock them over. Most of the time, bomb victims are initially unaware of what hit them. In Esther 4 the shock waves of the king's edict that burst forth upon the Persian Empire finally reverberated within the walls of the palace. Now they bowl over Esther herself.

The scene begins with Mordecai showing up at the palace gate dressed like a Halloween scarecrow: "When Mordecai learned all that had been done, he tore his clothes, put on sackcloth and ashes, and went out into the midst of the city and wailed loudly and bitterly" (Esther 4:1). Imagine it for a moment—Mordecai wearing a loose-fitting, dark-colored coarse garment made of goat's hair and hanging on him like a large gunnysack. On top of that, he has thrown ashes from a fire all over himself. He appears ghastly and unclean as he wails loudly and incessantly. Bitterly he moans and groans, flailing his arms and staggering as if demon-possessed. Mordecai held nothing back. It was a vivid expression of grief.

When Esther's maidens and eunuchs brought her the news, she too found herself caught up in a seizure of agony. Even before she knew what was happening, she convulsed in a genuine fit of personal anguish (verse 4). Deep down, Esther sensed something serious must have happened. Such behavior was not normal for Mordecai.

Through their back-and-forth exchange via one of the king's servants, Esther finally learned the shocking truth about Haman's plan. Mordecai gave her inside information about all that had happened, even down to the specifics regarding the exact amount of money in the deal and the date marked off on the calendar. He also sent along official evidence—a copy of the text of the edict (verses 5-8). "Have your queen read this," he said to the messenger. "It was signed with the king's signet ring." Mordecai carefully covered all the bases. He wanted to make sure Esther understood it was no rumor, but deadly real.

Not only was Mordecai careful with the information he communicated, he appealed to Esther to do something about it. He asked "her to go in to the king to implore his favor and to plead with him for her people" (verse 8). After all, she was queen and should have had an inside track. She was their people's only way out.

But Esther balked!

"All the king's servants and the people of the king's provinces know," she said, "that for any man or woman who comes to the king to the inner court who is not summoned, he has but one law, that he be put to death, unless the king holds out to him the golden scepter so that he may live. And I have not been summoned to come to the king for these thirty days" (verse 11).

Esther's first reaction was a negative one based on the fact that palace protocol forbade her to follow Mordecai's instructions. If she violated it, she could die. The gist of her three-part argument ran something like this: 1. You can't just walk in on the king. To enter the king's inner court without prior invitation means sure death for anyone. Everyone knows that! 2. The only exception to instant death is the king's special mercy and favor shown by extending his golden scepter. But who wants to take that chance? 3. The king hasn't even invited me to see him for 30 days. In other words, "my favor with the king has greatly waned. Although I am queen, I may have no influence unless Ahasuerus's heart is changed toward me and his favor is renewed." It wasn't as if Esther would be seeing Ahasuerus that night before they went to bed. They wouldn't be sitting at supper or reading in bed before the lights went out so she could just kind of say, "By the way honey, I . . ." No. It didn't work that way.

While it all made sense, Esther was essentially voicing her own fear and unwillingness to take a full stand on behalf of her people.

Mordecai realized that Esther was scared out of her wits. Who wouldn't be? He knew her real fear was revealing her identity, letting everyone know she was a Jew. So he argued with her.[3] Mordecai countered in three significant statements that, if acted upon, could alter the history of the Jews or her personal destiny. He read into Esther's reaction a strong orientation to self-preservation—that she wanted first and foremost to save her own life. Thus he warned her against thinking that she would remain safe and secure within the palace.[4] "Do not imagine," he said, "that you . . . can escape any more than all the Jews" (verse 13). You have no better chance of survival than any other Jew in the empire.

Then he stated, "For if you remain silent at this time, relief and deliverance will arise for the Jews from another place and you and your father's house will perish" (verse 14). Let there be no doubt about it— God will deliver His people. But if you remain silent, both you and your father's house will perish. You and your family will become extinct, while God's work will go on no matter what.

It's interesting to note at this point that Esther exhibited realistic feelings of fear. She saw no solution except to compromise, keep quiet, and put even more distance between her and her people. Interestingly the narrator passes no judgment on Esther's initial reluctance to stand up in behalf of her people. The story is so true-to-life! Esther was human. When the pressure comes down on us in life in a way that threatens our security, we're afraid too. So it was with Esther. Being brave is easy when we're protected and secure, when we don't have anything to risk.[5] Now Esther had everything to risk.

She was afraid to reveal who she really was, afraid to identify with her people.

"You can't escape it," Mordecai asserted. "And if you keep quiet, you will perish anyway." So it happens in every age. How often God's people find themselves in such situations. It is the case with many of us even today and will be apparent again during Jacob's "time of trouble" in the end. Whenever God's people are fearful of becoming involved or taking a stand or showing their true colors, they place themselves at an even greater risk. They cannot escape becoming involved. If they remain in a compromising situation, they will perish.

Again I want to say that the narrator does not condemn Esther's initial reluctance to stand for her people. He simply reports the story. The same is true with the apparent moral and spiritual compromises in Esther's life. The author does not criticize her questionable lifestyle choices. He simply creates a provocative image of that sad reality. Even then, he doesn't say clearly or in any great detail exactly what those compromises were. He leaves it to our imagination to fill in the blanks. In so doing, he draws us into the story in such a way that we confront not only the moral and spiritual principles at play, but, with the reality of our own fear, our own compromises as well.

The book of Esther isn't concerned with the picky details of what Esther compromised at—or what we might be compromising at, for that matter. The point of the story is to create not guilt, but moral and spiritual conviction. Biblical narratives engage us existentially and can deeply inform our moral life.[6] The story of God's redemptive work casts a moral vision upon our moral intelligence. And so do the stories of the people of the Bible. As Burton writes: "The ethical interest of stories does not lie in general moral principles which become evident—rather it lies in the interplay of such principles with the flawed character of the protagonists in the stories, producing complex actions in which we can recognize our own moral dilemmas and obligations."[7]

Finally, Mordecai asked, "Who knows whether you have not attained royalty [come to the palace] for such a time as this?" (verse 14). The basic meaning of the Hebrew word ʿēt involves time conceived as an opportunity or season. It is a space of time or an appointed time implying some kind of response or answer to the spiritual/moral realities of the moment.[8]

"Who knows if you have come to the throne for just such a time as this?" is probably one of the deepest theological statements of the book of Esther.[9] It hints at a larger picture that incorporates the seemingly isolated events of our lives. For Esther, the time had come for her to find out whether or not her selection as queen was simply a social accident. Now, perhaps, she could witness, in her own experience, the mystery of a hidden God who works within history for the preservation of His people—in spite of where they might be in terms of faithfulness to Him.[10]

Mordecai's words go down in history as one of those unforgettable turning-point speeches. It is one of those exhortations that make a critical difference in a person's life, because someone puts things into succinct perspective.

When the victorious Nazi armies stood poised on the shores of Normandy, ready to invade England during the darkest hour of World War II, only the stout heart of England's bulldog-faced prime minister, Winston Churchill, barred the way. Many think that his speech to Parliament on June 4, 1940, was the turning point of the war. "We shall go on to the end . . . we shall fight on the seas and oceans, we shall fight with growing confidence and growing strength in the air, we shall defend our island, whatever the cost may be, we shall fight on the beaches, we shall fight on the landing grounds, we shall fight in the fields and in the streets, we shall fight in the hills; we shall never surrender."[11]

It was a defining moment. Words do make a difference.

And it is the kind of message Mordecai sent to Esther: "This is your hour. *Stand. Speak! Die!* But whatever you do, *don't be silent.*"[12] "Now is the time to speak up, unfurl your colors, and stand for your people."

I want you to notice Mordecai's newfound boldness. Remember he, too had carefully hidden—or just didn't openly express—his own ethnic identity or faith. Like many lukewarm Jews of the Exile, he had faded into the woodwork and had gotten caught up living the good life of Persia. There came a defining moment, as we have seen, when Mordecai literally stared evil in the face in the person of Haman. When confronted with all that Haman symbolized, he grasped moral/spiritual issues in a new way. It was a moment in which he knew deep down inside that he had to act. Now was his chance—now or never. He felt compelled to step out and reveal his identity. Mordecai had to be outwardly who he was inside.

At this moment, then, we see how his decision to own his own identity and refuse to bow to Haman has actually emboldened him. He can now press Esther to make the same kind of decision. "How about it, Esther? What will it be? Will you too stand up and be counted? It's time to unfurl your colors. Own your identity. I have." No longer does he tell Esther to keep quiet, something he'd been doing for years. Obviously, it is not the Mordecai we have seen earlier in the story. It shows us how whenever we make a decision to follow God, do what is right because it's the right thing to do, He emboldens us spiritually and morally. Shortly we'll learn how this same principle came to reality in Esther's life as well. Once she shakes her spiritual lethargy and accepts her identity as a daughter of the living God, she finds herself filled with power and confidence. This newfound boldness that comes with moral decision is more than psychological. It results from our saying yes to the Holy Spirit's work in our life.

God's grace in our lives can take us—spiritually flabby, morally thin, lukewarm, disconnected from God or His people, caught up in the world—and actually strengthen us and with each step of the way make us become stronger and bolder and more committed than ever before. That's the wonderful story of Esther!

The Courage to Be

One of the burning questions Robert Coles had in mind when he visited Ruby Bridges was What secret spring do people like Ruby Bridges drink from when the moment comes for them to act in the face of danger and trouble? Where do we get the inclination to turn our backs on safety and comfort and do the very thing we are afraid to do? Where do we get that kind of energy, passion, and courage?

Coles says that he had no luck with explaining Ruby Bridges' indomitable courage in accepted psychiatric terms. A comment made by a White schoolteacher, however, caught his attention. She related what she saw one morning when Ruby walked into school: "A woman spat at Ruby but missed; Ruby smiled at her. A man shook his fist at her; Ruby smiled at him. Then she walked up the stairs, and she stopped and turned and smiled one more time! You know what she told one of the marshals? She told him she prays for those people, the ones in the mob, every night before she goes to sleep."[13]

The reference to prayer led Coles to examine Ruby's churchgoing practices. He began to realize how much our courage is linked to our sense of self-identity (who we are) in moral/spiritual realms. Like the Jewish children Els Ungvari worked to save during World War II. Els was just 23 in 1940 when she was in Rotterdam training as a social worker. She was attached to an orphanage where, among others, a number of Jewish children lived. That year the Nazis stormed Holland, and Els joined the Dutch underground. Because of her earlier experience with Jewish children, it assigned her to Amsterdam. There the Nazis herded up Jewish families to wait for freight trains that would take them to concentration camps in the east. Her job was to persuade terrified Jewish parents to turn over their children to her. She would then take them by train three at a time to the neighborhood of Nymegen, where the underground would hide them in a monastery. Some of the parents refused, and took their children with them to die. Others, who had a hunch what was in store for them, entrusted their little ones to Els and went on to die without them.

On the train the Jewish children could have at any time exposed Els. Abi dropped his pants and displayed his circumcision, a sure giveaway in a country where no male Gentile was circumcised. Alex blurted to a man in the next seat: "I'm Jewish. Are you Jewish too?" Hannah was making a fuss and was told to settle down: "Why?" she pouted. "It isn't Shabbat today."

Els made it to war's end, working in the underground until the liberation of Holland.[14] What intrigues me is the sense of identity Abi and Alex and Hannah had. They saw themselves in clear contrast to the larger world. It was hard for them to keep from revealing to others who they really were.

In his book *The Courage to Be* existentialist theologian Paul Tillich suggests that an understanding of courage presupposes an understanding of *being*. Courage and identity are linked. Tillich sees ethical and ontological notions behind the human phenomenon of courage. "The courage to be is the ethical act in which man affirms his own being."[15] While courage has many faces—you can show courage by advancing or by retreating, by dying or living for a good cause, by throwing off your yoke or by bearing it—at bottom it has to do with a sense of *being*. Who I am. What I really value deep down inside. Where I place myself in moral space. Whom I identify with.

Esther's dilemma was one of identity—of *being*. Who was she, really? Who were her people? Who was her God? Mordecai had asked "her to go in to the king to implore his favor and to plead with him for *her* people" (Esther 4:8). Esther's biggest obstacle wasn't going in to the king—it was revealing her identity. Until she fully owned that identity, Esther would never have had what it takes to reveal herself and to put her life on the line for what was right. For five years she'd been caught in the middle. The lure of Persian culture and life had thrown her sense of self off balance, creating another, almost virtual self. A self detached from the living God. Mordecai's earlier counsel to keep quiet hadn't helped.

But now Esther had only a brief slice of time to weigh Mordecai's counsel. When we've been accustomed to keeping our faith private, or when we've been absorbed in our world and its sphere of influence, it is difficult to shift gears, adjust our focus, and take a visible stand for God, for truth—for right. But Mordecai's strong exhortation became for Esther words of empowerment that challenged her to fulfill her destiny. In the midst of this defining moment, any sense of disconnection Esther may have felt between herself and her people—her faith and her God—once and for all dissolved. Esther, the young woman of dignity, grace, and beauty, became a person of great courage, strength, authority, and purpose. Why? She owned her identity. As such, her compliance with Mordecai's challenge was a considerable moral victory.[16]

In that defining moment Esther changed from fear to faith, from compromise to courage, from evading faith to declaring it. Ironically, Esther found her personal hour of decision to be a moment of finding herself. More important, she opened the way to experience God in a new and exciting way. Walter Anderson asserts that "courage is a three-letter word—and that word is *yes.*"[17] Esther finally and fully said yes to God.

From that moment of self-discovery Esther changed, never to be the same again.[18] As Eugene Peterson writes, "wherever there is a people of God there are enemies of God. . . . A realization that there is, in fact, an *enemy* forces a reassessment of priorities. The function of Haman . . . is to force a decision on the 'one thing needful.' The moment Haman surfaced, Esther began to move from being a beauty queen to becoming a Jewish saint, from being an empty-headed sex symbol to being a passionate intercessor, from the busy-indolent life in the harem to the high-risk venture of speaking for and identifying with God's people."[19]

As with Mordecai, resisting evil had to do with revealing her identity. It meant letting those around her know who she really was, where she stood, and what she believed, i.e., where God was in her life and how she related to His will. For Mordecai, resisting evil had to do with taking a personal stand because of religious/moral principle. He understood and acted on spiritual/moral issues before any crisis hit. For Esther, however, resisting evil came at a moment of unthinkable crisis—an unnerving incident of decision that she had to promptly make under the dreadful threat of impending holocaust. Both Mordecai and Esther awakened from their enchantment with Persian life. When the stakes became clear, Esther picked up faith and marched forward, grasping opportunity. Something deep within her heart transferred to her feet. Esther's response to Mordecai is both an acceptance of her destiny and a confession of faith that God can and will use her.

So it will be with God's people in the end. As with Esther and Mordecai, the foremost issue in that day will be one of identity. The people of God will make their irrevocable choice based on who they really are deep down inside their private innermost world. The question will then be Do God's professed people (in their heart of hearts) identify with the kingdom of the living God and the unnegotiable truths of His Word, or do they see themselves as part of the bewitching realities of a fallen world?

Unquestionably, it is God who graciously engineers these kinds of defining moments in the lives of His people. Jack Hayford describes a turning point as "a divinely engineered moment when life's focus shifts from self or trivia, and mind, emotion, and spirit are suddenly fastened to purpose in an indissoluble union; a crossover in spiritual life and meaning which brings full answer to one's life-mission."[20] Will we put our lives on the line for what is right? We never will until we know who we are. God is committed to helping define our moral/spiritual identity. The same God who presses us into such defining moments will likewise fit us for them.

I want to make something clear. The view of self-identity envisioned here is not merely some humanistic existential sense of *being* (as per Tillich), but self-surrender to God. Self-identity (understanding of *being*) and the courage it elicits, at bottom, have to do with surrender to God. Self-identity is relational—something between oneself and God. Nor is courage a humanistic bravado "I'll lay myself down" ("If I perish, I perish!"). Mordecai's words to Esther, "Who knows whether you have not attained royalty for such a time as this?" (Esther 4:14), show deference to God's ultimate sovereign control. Esther's response, "I will go . . . and if I perish, I perish" (verse 16), indicates self-surrender to that control. Courage and identity are linked in the context of self-surrender to a sovereign God.

Once again the story of Esther brings us *behind the seen:*

Behind the seen is a confused and terrified heart.

Behind the seen is a defining moment of personal destiny.

Behind the seen is a God who graciously pushes His people to the brink, knowing that in that defining moment of personal destiny they find their true identity and are emboldened to live for Him with a renewed passion.

Sooner or later God offers each of us a moment for courage. We will all stand at the crossroad sometime. And when we get there we shall have to decide whether we will do the right thing, even if it means putting our lives on the line. No one can decide for us. They can teach us, inspire us, threaten us. But no one can act in our place. Each of us must finally do it alone in keeping with our point of reference, our sense of being, our self-identity. When those moments come, we can be sure of the words of Hanani the prophet to King Asa: "For the eyes of the Lord move to and fro throughout the earth that He may strongly support those whose heart is completely His" (2 Chron. 16:9).

---

[1] Robert Coles, *The Moral Life of Children* (Boston: The Atlantic Monthly Press, 1986), pp. 12-27.

[2] "The Deal Makers," *Newsweek* (Nov. 2, 1998): pp. 22-28; "Inside Wye Plantation," *Time* (Nov. 2, 1998): pp. 38-44.

[3] A. M. Rodríguez, *Esther: A Theological Approach*, p. 69.

[4] A. B. Luter and B. C. Davis, *God Behind the Seen*, p. 230.

[5] Rodríguez, p. 69.

[6] John Burton, *Ethics and the Old Testament* (Harrisburg, Penn.: Trinity Press International, 1997), p. 34.

[7] *Ibid.*, p. 36. This is not an either/or statement. Biblical narratives do generate general moral principles that become evident and normative, but the author does not present them as abstract generalizing notions with no parameters or in isolation from real life. Scripture always roots them in concrete moral exigencies of real life.

[8] "'ēt,'" *Theological Wordbook of the Old Testament,* ed. R. Laird Harris (Chicago: Moody Press, 1980), vol. 2, pp. 679-691. The LXX usually uses the Greek word *kairos* (198 times) to translate this Hebrew word for time ("Kairos," *The New International Dictionary of New Testament Theology,* ed. Colin Brown [Grand Rapids: Zondervan Pub. House, 1971], vol. 3, p. 835).

[9] Rodríguez, p. 25.

[10] *Ibid.*

[11] Sir Winston Churchill, speech on Dunkirk, House of Commons, June 4, 1940.

[12] C. R. Swindoll, *Esther: A Woman of Strength and Dignity,* p. 85.

[13] Coles, pp. 22, 23.

[14] Lewis B. Smedes, *A Pretty Good Person* (San Francisco: Harper and Row, Publishers, 1990), pp. 48, 49.

[15] Paul Tillich, *The Courage to Be* (New Haven: Yale University Press, 1952), p. 3.

[16] J. G. McConville, *Ezra, Nehemiah, and Esther* (Philadelphia: Westminster Press, 1985), p. 172.

[17] Walter Anderson, *Courage Is a Three-Letter Word* (New York: Random House, 1986), p. 12.

[18] J. W. Hayford, *Redemption and Restoration,* p. 112.

[19] Eugene Peterson, *Five Smooth Stones for Pastoral Work* (Atlanta: John Knox Press, 1980), pp. 172, 173.

[20] Hayford, p. 112.

CHAPTER SIX

SACRED HOOPS—WHEN BEING AWARE IS MORE IMPORTANT THAN BEING SMART

Esther 4:13-5:5

Serious fans of basketball know that the Chicago Bulls are the greatest team in basketball history. They have twice won three consecutive championships. In the process they became one of the twentieth-century's sports icons.

You might think that the Bulls' success would consist of just two words: Michael Jordan. Any team led by Michael Jordan was sure to reach the World Championship. Right? Of course, it is true that he could do things on the basketball court that no one else had ever approached. As Los Angeles Laker superstar Magic Johnson would say, "there's Michael and there's all the rest of us." The Bulls, though, were a team, and not just one player. They won their two three-straight championships without either a dominant center or an all-star point guard, because all the players worked together toward the same goal, sacrificing themselves for the betterment of the team. In fact, some persuaded Jordan to score fewer points so the Bulls could become less "Jordan-centric" and achieve team success.

How did the ego-driven likes of Michael Jordan, Scottie Pippen, Toni Kukoc, Dennis Rodman, and other members of the Bulls ever surrender the "Me" for the "We"? It took one of the most successful coaches in NBA history and an innovative paradigm of leadership. Bulls coach Phil Jackson reveals the secret in his memoirs *Sacred Hoops.*[1] According to Jackson, there's "more to basketball than basketball." There's Zen Buddhism, sacred Lakota teachings, meditation, and compassion toward rival players. The son of Pentecostal preachers (both Dad and Mom), Jackson rebelled against his strict religious upbringing by adopting an array of Eastern and Native American spiritual disciplines. His dream was not just to win basketball championships. He wanted to do it in a way that wove together his two greatest passions: basketball and spiritual exploration. And so the path to repeated world championship combined highly developed athletic skill and quietness and meditation—in which players emptied their minds of the endless jabbering of thoughts so that their body could do instinctively what it had been trained to do without the mind getting in the way.

In short, the way of the Bulls was "mindful awareness." The team had regular meditation moments integrated into their practice. They formed a spiritual hoop as it were around the secular hoop they so passionately pursued—hence the title of his book. The first time they practiced Jackson's meditation techniques, Michael Jordan thought the coach was joking. Midway through the session he cocked one eye open and took a glance around the room to see if any of his teammates were actually doing it. To his surprise, many of them were.

Jackson attempted to create an environment in which his players could learn to play with a clear mind and stay focused in the midst of chaos. Awareness is everything, Jackson writes. "Being aware is more important than being smart." And so you have to still your soul, quiet your mind. Tune out your jabbering thoughts and the chaos taking place in your world. Only then can you effectively play the game.

A grand pause takes place between chapters 4 and 5 of the ancient book of Esther. A time-out, it is a 72-hour intermission that represents a silent yet powerful interlude during which Esther draws on the source of her strength. Between her decision, "Thus I will go in to the king, which is not according to the law; and if I perish, I perish" (Esther 4:16), and her action, "Now it came about on the third day that Esther put on her royal robes and stood in the inner court of the king's palace" (Esther 5:1), she enters a period of waiting. Three intentional days of deliberate listening, searching, "mindfulness." Of becoming aware of what God might be doing for His endangered people.

An important little Hebrew word helps us catch the point of this pause: *kēn*, translated *"thus, so, likewise"* in Esther 4:16. Its root meaning gives the idea of moving "from provision through preparation and establishment to fixity and rightness." The word expresses a progression from unpreparedness to fixed readiness. Most of the time we simply translate it as "prepare." In view of something in the future, I do certain things now in order to get ready for it.[2] Surprisingly, *kēn* appears twice, back to back, in Esther's response to Mordecai—"I and my maidens also will fast *in the same way. And thus I will go*" (Esther 4:16, NASB). Back to back—*kēn ybeken*. In other words, "When this [period of preparation] is done, I will go" (NIV). Something important must first take place. Only then will Esther be prepared to act.

Sacred Hoops

As Esther ponders Mordecai's words, "And who knows whether you have not attained royalty for such a time as this?" (verse 14), she wonders, *Is this so? Is God about to do something through me? If so, I need to know. I need to be ready.* Remember, Esther was a good person. She believed in God. The problem was that God just wasn't the all-encompassing priority of her life. She was part of the compromising Diaspora of exiled Jews. Now, in view of the coming crisis, her focus shifts, and she does what it takes both to deepen her relationship with God and to be truly aware of His leading—if, in fact, He is leading.

It reminds me of what I've heard many inactive members say through the years: "I left the church, but I never left God. God has always been a part of my life, even though I don't go to church or do all the things the church tells me to do." While their lifestyle, personal decisions, and priorities may not harmonize with the way God asks them to live or be or do, in their heart of hearts these inactive members still believe. They still consider themselves one of God's children and feel very much in tune with Him. But you know, when a crisis breaks out, when life fills up with chaos, many of those same people discover that they're not as connected to God as they once imagined. Esther now realized that she'd been running on empty and did something about it. She could not act without first quieting her soul and connecting once again with God, without first clarifying the issues and what God might be up to. It is a picture of how it will be with many of God's Laodicean people in the end. The book of Esther is the story of a loving God who wakes up His people before it is too late. When many begin to sense the looming crisis of the end-time, they, too, will do the important heart work that prepares them for what God wants to do for them and through them.

"Awareness is everything," Phil Jackson asserts in *Sacred Hoops*. What did that mean for Esther? It meant, first of all, restoring her connection with the people of God—owning her spiritual/moral identity. That's exactly what Esther did in a very practical way. "Go gather all the Jews . . . and fast for me," she commanded Mordecai (verse 16, NKJV). It's easy to race by simple phrases such as this and miss their subtle meaning. One of the forms of the Hebrew word translated here as *gather* means to *wrap* as in a cover.[3] Isaiah writes of a bed that is too short on which to stretch out on, and a blanket too small to wrap oneself in (Isa. 28:20). Esther uses the same word: gather, wrap. What was she saying? "Gather them together and let me be wrapped (as in a cover) in the sphere of their collective intercession." Esther identifies with her people, wraps herself within what it means not only to be Jewish but God's people. "This is what I believe. These are my people, my community of faith. These are the things God asks me to do for Him. This is how I am to live in the world. It is who I am."

You will remember that Esther has been a compromising, lukewarm follower of God. He had revealed lots of things to her and her people that both she and they were not living or experiencing. Perhaps she didn't think some of those things were all that important and was just cruising along, enjoying the good life. But now, when Esther says to "go gather all the Jews and have them begin praying for me," she owns her identity, wrapping herself in it. She formed a "sacred hoop," moving from the "Me" to the "We," and in doing so deepened her awareness of God and His presence.

Esther shows that spiritual renewal and spiritual power in times of crisis do not center in individualism. They come in the context of community with the people of God. When we want to get back on track with God we need to step once again into the sphere of His body. Detaching ourselves from His people, we lose connection with God. Thus when we forget the "We" and fling out into the "Me" we discard our sense of identity, and our moral spiritual life begins to decay.

God has designed that we find spiritual and moral power in community. In that moment of crisis Esther instinctively understood this relational principle.

So Esther unfurls her colors and identifies with her people and her faith: "Go, assemble all the Jews" and have them "fast for me" (Esther 4:16); "let my life be given me as my petition, and my people as my request" (Esther 7:3); "for we have been sold, I and my people" (verse 4); "now if we . . . , I" (verse 4); "how can I endure to see the calamity which shall befall my people, and how can I endure to see the destruction of my kindred?" (Esther 8:6).

Awareness for Esther also meant sensing God's presence and being in touch with what God was doing in the world. It meant becoming awake to God and attentive to His will and His way of doing things, then focusing on His priorities and being in touch with His timing. It led to her three-day fast—72 hours of mindfulness (Esther 4:16).

The book of Esther mentions fasting several times. The Old Testament often associates fasting with prayer and deep religious feelings (2 Sam. 12:16; Ps. 35:13; Jonah 3:5-9; Dan. 9:3).[4] The Jews didn't fast to lose weight, but rather for spiritual reasons. When an issue became a prominent concern in their lives, it was no time for fun and feasting. It was an occasion for prayer and mindfulness. Fasting and prayer are a preparatory experience during which we gain perspective on what we are dealing with. They provide an interlude in life in which we exchange our weakness for God's strength. A pause that enables us to hear God's voice more clearly. The word for fasting literally means "to cover the mouth." During fasting we symbolically cover the entrances or accesses to our innermost being. Covering the eyes and ears of our mind, we filter what enters our heart. Fasting renews spiritual vision. As with Esther, when you feel that your life is out of control or that you have lost your first love for the Lord, fasting can help you focus once again on God's plan for your life.

Before refrigerators people used ice to preserve food. During winter, when streams and lakes froze, people cut large blocks of ice and hauled them to icehouses for storage. Later they would sell the ice to customers who would use it in their iceboxes or coolers. Icehouses had thick insulated walls, no windows, and a tightly fitted door. When the workers brought blocks of ice to the icehouse, they covered them with sawdust. It kept them from freezing together and added further insulation. The ice in icehouses would often last well into the summer.

One man lost a valuable pocket watch while working in an icehouse. He searched diligently for it, carefully raking through the sawdust, but didn't find it. His fellow workers joined his search, but their efforts, too, proved unsuccessful. During their noon break a small boy overheard the men talking about the lost watch. While they were eating, he slipped into the icehouse and soon emerged with the watch, to the men's amazement. "How did you find it?" they asked in puzzled surprise.

"I closed the door," the boy replied, "lay down in the sawdust, and kept very still. Soon I heard the watch ticking."

Often the question is not whether God is speaking to us or working in our lives. He is always revealing Himself. The issue, rather, is whether we are being still enough, quiet enough, aware enough to hear God and understand what it is He is saying about our life. When we wait, we listen, and when we listen, we become aware of God's voice and are more inclined to let Him lead. Waiting upon God in prayer and fasting in unpredictable and unprecedented situations is crucial. At such times His Word becomes a powerful point of contact between ourselves and God.

In his book *Experiencing God* Henry Blackaby writes: "If you do not have clear instructions from God in a matter, pray and wait. Learn patience. Depend on God's timing. His timing is always right and best. Don't get in a hurry. He may be withholding directions to cause you to seek Him more intently. Don't try to skip over the relationship to get on with *doing*."[5] Did you catch that? "Don't skip over the relationship to get to the *doing*." Make sure *relationship* comes before *doing*. Only then can you be sure your *doing* is in keeping with God's plan and timing.

Jesus says, "He who belongs to God hears what God says. The reason you do not hear is that you do not belong to God" (John 8:47, NIV). Esther knew she could hear what God had to say only when she truly quieted herself before Him—belonged to Him more than ever before in her life. She determined to wait on the Lord and allow Him to guide her thoughts and frame her words. As a result she resolved to submit, wait, watch, and finally, join God in whatever He was already doing or was about to do.[6]

Blackaby further notes: "We often act as though God tells us what He wants us to do and sends us off all by ourselves to try and do it. Then, at any time we need Him we can call Him, and He will help us. That is never the biblical picture. When He is about to do something, He reveals what He is about to do to His people. He wants to do it through His people."[7] As Esther prepared to go before the king, she had to wait, think, pray, stay quiet, fast, and listen to God's voice in her soul. Only then could God work through her.

Banquets Are My Thing

Because Esther stopped to focus on her relationship with God before she did anything else, she was able to approach the moment of truth—to step into the presence of the king—calmly and wisely and confidently: "On the third day Esther put on her royal robes and stood in the inner court of the palace, in front of the king's hall. The king was sitting on his royal throne in the hall, facing the entrance. When he saw Queen Esther standing in the court, he was pleased with her and held out to her the gold scepter that was in his hand. So Esther approached and touched the tip of the scepter" (Esther 5:1, 2, NIV).

Esther walked into his presence with confidence. She didn't cringe or cower, but simply stood there in full view. Though she was doing something she'd never done before—something against palace protocol that could have cost her her life—she stood tall and confident in the Lord. When Ahasuerus saw her in the court, Esther obtained favor in his sight. He extended his golden scepter to her. Remember, without that gesture from the king, she would have died. But no, he held out the scepter, and Esther approached the throne. She reached out and touched the scepter's tip, making personal connection with the king.

Esther didn't know what to expect. But then Ahasuerus didn't know what she wanted either. After all, Esther's actions are unprecedented. So he asked the obvious: "What's on your mind, Esther?

What's troubling you?" No doubt he sensed that something really important must be weighing on her heart for her to take such a personal risk. In fact, he goes further. "What can I do for you?" he asks. "Name it. There's no limit. It's yours!" (see verse 3).

What would you do? No doubt this is her moment to bring the roof down on Haman. To tell it all. But she doesn't. Not now. Esther doesn't point a finger at Haman. Nor does she play on Ahasuerus's emotions or try to manipulate him by bursting into tears, falling down in front of him, and whining about the looming destruction of her and her people. Calmly she says, without hysteria or sobs or nervous voice, "I've planned a banquet, and I'd love to have you and Haman attend" (see verse 4).

"Great idea," the king replies. "Banquets are my thing!" Esther knew that. By the time we're through reading Esther we will have noted the 10 banquets that distinguish the little book. Yes, banquets were the king's thing. And Esther knew it. "Then the king said, 'Bring Haman quickly that we may do as Esther desires.' So the king and Haman came to the banquet which Esther had prepared" (verse 5)

Isn't that incredible? While Esther had been fasting, she'd also been preparing a banquet. As she waited on the Lord, "God was at work in the waiting, filling her thoughts with a plan."[8] How does God speak when we sit quietly before Him, waiting, listening? *Esther, give a banquet. Esther, invite Haman. And here's what you need to say . . .* It was the still small voice of God heard in a stilled heart, the Spirit working upon human imagination. Amazing, isn't it?

Later during that banquet we can imagine Esther sitting there and musing, *Isn't God great! I could have lost my head. Instead, here they are at this banquet I've prepared. The plan is working beautifully. What a surprise!*

But the plot thickens. As they're sipping wine at the banquet, Ahasuerus, too, is thinking to himself, *Something's troubling her. Something must be wrong. Esther would never have risked coming into my presence as she did unless she had a very good reason.*

So between drinks, while they're sipping wine, he raises the matter again. "What can I do for you? Just ask, and I will give you as much as half of my kingdom" (verse 6, CEV). "Come on, tell me what it is!"

"My petition and my request is this," Esther replied. "If the king regards me with favor and if it pleases the king to grant my petition and fulfill my request, let the king and Haman come tomorrow to the banquet I will prepare for them. Then I will answer the king's question" (verse 7, NIV).

I want you to catch what Esther has just done. She could have done everything today that she's going to do tomorrow. But something prompted her to put it off. Something didn't seem quite right. I don't think she went into that first banquet with a fixed plan. Remember, she's just spent three days in earnest waiting on the Lord and developing a mindfulness that put her in touch with God's leading. She's trusting God's timing on this one. Thus tuned into the moment, she feels that now doesn't seem like the right time.

In *Sacred Hoops* Jackson says the greatest thing is awareness. "What you really need to do is become more acutely aware of what's happening right now, *this very moment.*" [9] You have to clear the mind and live being aware of what is happening at that very moment. Then and only then can your instinctive response be appropriate. Now, how does this work?

I've never been very good at fast-action team sports. Years ago I played a game of basketball with an energetic group of men from the church I pastored. Early on in the game someone passed me the ball, but before I knew what had happened, another person picked it off. Again the ball came my way, but I barely caught it, and my response was too slow. I never saw the ball again during that game. The game was moving faster than I could think—faster than my responses. It was as if I had to stop and look at the ball, saying to myself, "Yeah! This is a basketball. Now, where's the net? What do I do with it now?" Because I was concentrating on a specific skill I had not carefully honed, I was not prepared for the demands of the moment. I wasn't ever sure what was going on.

The same is true when I shoot skeets at a local gun club. It's amazing watching some of the shooters who have been years at this fast-paced sport. Whether they come out high or low, from the left or right, toward you or away from you, they instantly pulverize with a blast of 12-gauge shot the circular clay targets accelerating out from any of the skeet houses. Experienced shooters have a trained eye and reflexes. They know their distances and angles and how far to shoot either ahead or above the climbing target. To a less experienced shooter like me it seems as if they do it without aiming. I was raised on a farm where target practicing was a regular part of family entertainment. I can nail any fixed target dead on. But the world of moving targets is another thing. I've discharged many a round of shot in the air at nothing—so it seems. My problem is that by force of habit, I aim at the flying skeets as I would a fixed target. I'm too intentional, too deliberate. By the time I pull the trigger the target is long gone. "It's instinctive," they say. "You just have to see what's happening and gauge yourself at the moment." It takes hours of practice to come to that level of shooting.

A similar thing happens with driving. When we first learn to drive, our mind concentrates on every detail. We're making decisions about every moment. Right foot on gas, left on clutch or brake. We're busy looking ahead while making sure we know what's coming up behind as we try to gauge how much to turn the steering wheel to the left or to the right. During those early moments we overcompensate. Our moves are jerky, uncertain, imprecise, and we drive slowly, deliberately. But with time that all changes, and it becomes intuitive. We can talk, adjust seats, speak on cell phones, and drive at high speeds all at the same time. When we have to make a split-second decision we instinctively know what to do.

This is what has happened with Esther. Tuned in to God, she was acutely aware of what was happening right then. She had spent time listening, waiting, becoming open to His promptings. So she says, "There's something I do want to say to you, but I want to wait till tomorrow." For some reason, as we'll soon learn, God's timing required one more day. Had Esther blurted things out just then, it would have compromised an important part of God's unfolding plan. Jackson is right when he states, "What you really need to do is become more acutely aware of what's happening right now, *this very moment*." For Christians, that means being still and knowing God's voice so well that they will recognize His leading at any moment.

God's incredible promise to His people working their way through difficult circumstances in their lives is "I will instruct you and teach you in the way which you should go; I will counsel you with My eye upon you" (Ps. 32:8). The wonderful promise is that right now God is working all around you and in your life. His eye is on you. The eye makes no sound when it moves. As Chuck Swindoll says, "it requires a sensitive earthly eye to watch the movement of the eye of God—God's directions."[10] But God promises to open our senses when we wait upon Him. Isaiah 30:20, 21 declares that "although the Lord has given you bread of privation and water of oppression, He, your Teacher will no longer hide Himself, but your eyes will behold your Teacher. And your ears will hear a word behind you, 'This is the way, walk in it,' whenever you turn to the right or to the left."

So often we jump ahead and do rash things, shooting from the hip, saying or doing things we later regret. But when we've waited sufficiently on the Lord, when He gets full control of our hearts, we're like a glove, and His hand is moving us wherever He pleases. That was Esther's experience. You can experience God in this way, too.

Living in the Meantime

Some time ago a friend of mine shared an incredible moment she had with a wealthy Jewish woman who came to her for therapy. During their session together my friend learned that her client had an extremely high anxiety level and was a high risk for suicide. Her mother had died of suicide at the age of 60. Now in her mid-50s, she was staring terminal cancer in the eye. In fact, she had as a last resort just spent $100,000 on a bone marrow transplant. It was following the bone marrow transplant that her anxiety level dramatically increased and she became suicidal. It had repulsed her when they injected her with the tissue from someone else's body.

Why did she react so to this procedure? my friend wondered to herself. *Was she afraid of AIDS? Perhaps it was the pain of the large needle plunging into her body.* "What was so repulsive about this procedure?" she finally asked the client.

She'll never forget the answer: "It is repulsive to me that I would need something from someone else to live."

A proud Jewish woman staring death in the face and offended that she needed help from anyone. So much so that she felt tempted to take her own life. What a graphic image of our human heart—when chaos fills our world, we want to go it alone. We detest the thought that we need help from outside ourselves. That our very existence depends on God.

Esther is the story of a woman and a people who finally came to a moment in their lives when they said, "I need God! We need God! The only way through this is with Him. We must first be still and wrap ourselves in the sacred hoop of His purposes and what it means to be His people. Quiet our heart to the place where we can not only know His voice, but hear Him speaking." That's how it will be with many of God's children in the crisis of the end.

But it speaks to us as well today. Right now may be one of those *in-between* moments in your own life. An anxiety-filled intermission. A 72-hour interlude between a decision and some required action. A period during which you may know what you need to do but not how to do it. You're like a little child who doesn't know how to go out or come in. Maybe there's chaos all around you as confusion, disappointment, and some looming crisis fills your life. Perhaps it's time for you to pray and to fast and to call upon a few close friends to fast and pray with you. Time to wrap yourself in a sacred hoop of intercession and fellowship in the body of Christ. Maybe you need to announce, "I'm not going to rush into this unpredictable and unprecedented moment on my own. I don't know my way through. I can't find the path to walk on. So I'm going to wait. In the meantime I'm going to give it to God and listen for Him with an sensitive ear. I'll watch for the Lord's leading."

If it is such a moment in your life, the same God who impressed Esther to throw a banquet and then delay her request one more day will lead you, too. You can be sure of it. God is trustworthy. He will lead, hear, and bless as you seek His face.

Knowing God's voice at such moments, though, is not a simple formula. It is not a prescribed method you can automatically follow without thinking. Knowing God's voice comes from an intimate love relationship with God, born out of heartfelt surrender to Him in prayer and obedience. Out of an intimate relationship with God, we come to recognize His voice. It is like tacit knowledge, understanding that we gain through experience. Inarticulate and intuitive, it can be best described in relation to people we have come to know in a personal way. The phone may ring and when you pick it up a familiar voice you may not have heard in years speaks, but as soon as you hear it, you know who it is. Or you're lying in bed at night and hear someone walking down the hallway. Through the years you've become accustomed to the familiar gait, and you instinctively know who it is. No one taught you these things. You didn't even consciously teach them to yourself. Instead, you just learned them by experience. And you are always right.

That's how it must be with God. Tacit. Intuitive. Developed through intimacy with Him so much so that you can always sense when He is at work around you, speaking, leading, working. As Blackaby notes: "If you have trouble hearing God speak, you are in trouble at the very heart of your Christian experience."[11] If this is true with you, it is time to fast and pray and fill your heart with the Word of God. It may be time, too, to obey where God has already spoken, to fulfill what you already know to be God's will for you.

A subtle but powerful link exists between obeying God and knowing God. God reveals Himself to His people by what He does, and our obedience opens the way for Him to work. Both Mordecai and Esther came to experience this fact. Because they obeyed, they saw God at work in keeping with their obedience. In the process they gained incredible, practical knowledge of God. When God works through us to accomplish His purpose, we come to know Him by experience. We also learn to know God when He meets a need in our life.

All this is buttressed, of course, by Scripture that validates whether or not our personal experience with God is consistent with the way He works.

Behind the seen is a meditative heart, wrapping itself in the sacred hoop of shared identity and petition.

Behind the seen is an alert heart, listening, waiting for God to reveal His plan. Ready to obey when the timing's right.

Behind the seen is one who graciously leads His attentive, obedient people through any crisis.

---

[1] Phil Jackson and Hugh Delehanty, *Sacred Hoops: Spiritual Lessons of a Hardwood Warrior* (New York: Hyperion, 1995).

[2] *"Kēn," Theological Wordbook of the Old Testament,* vol. 1, pp. 433, 434.

[3] *"Kānas," ibid.,* pp. 444, 445.

[4] R. K. Harrison, "Fast," *International Standard Bible Encyclopedia,* vol. 2, p. 284.

[5] Henry T. Blackaby and Claude V. King, *Experiencing God: Knowing and Doing the Will of God* (Nashville: LifeWay Press, 1990), p. 75.

[6] *Ibid.,* p. 28.

[7] *Ibid.,* p.19.

[8] C. R. Swindoll, *Esther: A Woman of Strength and Dignity,* p. 102.

[9] Jackson and Delehanty, p. 115.

[10] Swindoll, p. 99.

[11] Blackaby and King, p. 36.

CHAPTER SEVEN

WHEN LIFE ISN'T FAIR
AND HONOR IS YOUR SHAME

Esther 5:9 - 6:3

An old French folktale tells the story of two daughters—one rude and proud, the other courteous and gentle. The rude and proud daughter was her mother's favorite, while the courteous and gentle daughter was unjustly neglected, despised, and mistreated.

One day, while drawing water from the village well, the good daughter met a poor woman who asked for a drink. The girl responded with kind words and gave the woman a cup of water. The little girl's kindness and good manners so pleased the woman that she gave her a gift. "Each time you speak," said the woman, "a flower or jewel will come out of your mouth."

When the little girl got home, her mother began to scold her for taking so long to bring the water. When she started to apologize, two roses, two pearls, and two diamonds appeared out of her mouth. It astonished the mother. After hearing her daughter's story and seeing the number of beautiful jewels that accompanied the account, the mother called her other daughter and sent her off to get the same gift. The bad daughter, however, didn't want to be seen performing the lowly task of drawing water, so she grumbled sourly all the way to the well. When she reached the well, a beautiful queenly woman (the same woman as before) asked her for a drink. Disagreeable and proud, the girl responded rudely. As a result, she, too, received her reward. Each time she opened her mouth, snakes and toads leaped out.[1]

How's that for poetic justice? There's something in each one of us that longs for circumstances to be fair. Our inner sense of justice yearns for retribution for the cruel and greedy and reward for the gentle and kind of heart. Each culture dreams of the same pattern of justice. Maybe that's why folktales have always been so appealing. We want good people to receive their rewards and "live happily ever after," while bad people get soundly punished. Even as we read Esther those same thoughts cross our minds.

Chapters 5 and 6 of the book of Esther are poetic justice par excellence. Depicting a dramatic reversal, they set the upside-down cake before us with fascinating detail. Our journey through this potentially tragic story suddenly takes some ironic twists. We begin to sense the handwriting on the wall. In the process we confront the scandalous reality of honor and dishonor. Esther, though, is more than a folktale. It is about God's providential work to bring our greatest dream to reality.

A Vast and Tender Ego

Two episodes following Esther's first banquet focus fully on Haman. The first appears in chapter 5. "Then Haman went out that day glad and pleased of heart; but when Haman saw Mordecai in the king's gate, and that he did not stand up or tremble before him, Haman was filled with anger against Mordecai. Haman controlled himself, however, went to his house, and sent for his friends and his wife Zeresh. Then Haman recounted to them the glory of his riches, and the number of his sons, and every instance where the king had magnified him, and how he had promoted him above the princes and servants of the king. Haman also said, 'Even Esther the queen let no one but me come with the king to the banquet which she had prepared; and tomorrow also I am invited by her with the king. Yet all of this does not satisfy me every time I see Mordecai the Jew sitting at the king's gate.' Then Zeresh his wife and all his friends said to him, 'Have a gallows fifty cubits high made and in the morning ask the king to have Mordecai hanged on it, then go joyfully with the king to the banquet.' And the advice pleased Haman, so he had the gallows made" (verses 9-14).

Interestingly, Haman is unlike every other character in the story: we step into his mind. "His motives, drives, and attitudes are transparent." The narrator bares Haman's twisted soul.[2] He heads for home, full of himself, feeling on top of the world. His excitement is what we would call pure joy, ecstasy. His inflated ego is even more swollen when he leaves the exalted company of the king and queen. It was the ultimate opportunity to drop names. His place in the world is now certainly secure. Around him the people bow, giving witness to his greatness and power. So he walks out of the palace, bursting with pride and ego, riding on cloud nine, and runs straight into Mordecai—that Jew who will not respect him. I like the way Scripture records it: Mordecai "did not stand up or tremble before him" (verse 9).

He shows no outward compliance, no sign of fear, just a peaceful heart and firm resolution. That's what happens when you take a firm stand for what's right. So despite Haman's official status and power, despite his evil decree, Mordecai still remains unintimidated. As Haman leaves the palace, Mordecai doesn't look all that impressed. It devastates the Persian official. The Jew doesn't even fear him. Haman now realizes that the vengeance he has in store is not adequate, for it does not secure him the personal victory he needs. He has not forced Mordecai to recognize his power. If the man continues to defy him for the next 11 months, his defiance will endure as a victory that mere murder cannot expunge.[3]

Devastated, depressed, and furious, Haman heads for home. There he sends for his wife, Zeresh, and his friends and revels in his own glory. I want to stop right here and point out that the bottom-line theme in this series of episodes in chapters 5 and 6 concerns honor and dishonor. The word "honor" appears several times in the unfolding story (see Esther 6:3, 6, 7, 9, 11).

"Then Haman recounted to them the glory of his riches, and the number of his sons, and every instance where the king had magnified him, and how he had promoted him above the princes and servants of the king" (Esther 5:11). Can you imagine having to sit and listen to all this? Brag, brag, brag. Me, me, me. He tells them what he's worth and how many sons he's got, then goes over his promotions and opportunities. Finally Haman describes how he's gotten in with the queen. Scripture tells us that he told "every instance" that the king had magnified him (verse 11). Haman droned on and on and on. Of course nobody wanted to offend him. After all, he did have the king's signet ring.

But you know they had to be rolling their eyes and wondering, *When's this guy going to quit?* The bottom line is that Haman is caught up with self-honor, and self-honor is always scandalous, always demeaning, and always leaves one personally empty.

The interesting thing is that all his glory, wealth, power, opportunity didn't satisfy Haman. Mordecai's presence loomed over all his thoughts, robbing him of all pleasure he might have derived from the honor, wealth, and power in which he gloried.[4] "Yet all of this does not satisfy me," he sighed (verse 13).

Finally his wife piped up and said, in effect, "So why don't you shut up and do something about it? I'm sick and tired of hearing you moan and groan about this Mordecai." "Have a gallows fifty cubits high made and in the morning ask the king to have Mordecai hanged on it, then go joyfully with the king to the banquet" (verse 14).

Wonderful! Why didn't I think of that? Haman loved the idea and ordered the gallows built. Now, the "gallows" here are not what we traditionally think of—hanging by the neck on some rope till dead. No, the original word means "pole" or "stake." Like a sharpened pencil. In Persia, they didn't hang their victims with a rope—they impaled them. A stake was thrust into their body opening, and then the body suspended on it. It was an anguishing, humiliating, torturous death. In addition, the gallows Haman had built was 75 feet tall. That's seven and a half stories. Sounds like overkill, doesn't it? The extraordinarily high gallows represents the height to which Haman had risen in his own thinking. Upon it, the man who will not move before Haman will squirm. Since he will not bow, he shall hang.[5] Haman's anger now consumed him to the point where only the agonizing death of his enemy would satisfy him. He went to sleep that night listening to the thump and bump and pounding of the construction crew as they worked through the night, building the pole upon which his enemy would hang. Yet Mordecai is oblivious to his fate.

At this point in the story it's easy to wonder where God is. His people stand condemned to genocide. Mordecai, a leader among them, faces a more immanent death. Yet God remains silent. Is there any hope?

Sleepless in Susa

"Androclus and the Lion" is an ancient story that illustrates the un-expected results of an act of kindness. Recorded by Autus Gellius in *Noctes Attica* (Volume XV), it tells of a poor slave (Androclus) who ran away from his cruel Roman master. Androclus hid for weeks in the Italian forest. During this time he came upon a lion resting near the mouth of a cave. At first the animal frightened Androclus, but then he realized that the lion was in great pain, confused, and tired. A large sharp thorn protruded from a gash in one of its paws. Androclus spoke softly, stroking the lion's mane and back. He took the end of the thorn in his fingers; then gave a strong, quick pull, and out it came. The lion shuddered and groaned. Finally, it slept.

Just then the clouds let go, and it began to pour down rain. Androclus crawled into the cave and fell asleep. Minutes later he awoke as the lion crawled into the cave next to him, dragging its leg, and col-lapsed with a wheezing sigh. The cave was large, and the man and the beast lived together for several weeks until soldiers found Androclus one day scooping water from a stream. Forced back to the city, Androclus soon received the dreaded sentence most runaway slaves faced—death. Taken to the Colosseum, he was to be sport as a crowd would gleefully watch a hungry lion be let loose in the arena with him. The mob spat its hatred and a thunderous cheer went up when the an-imal keepers released a lion—a lion that had not eaten for several days, an animal poked and prodded into fierce anger by the soldiers. It roared when it saw Androclus, and bounded headlong toward its prey.

Androclus knew he didn't have a chance. Still, his muscles tensed for the fight, readied for pain. He waited for the weight of the animal, steel-ing against the first slashing blow. Instead of searing pain, he felt the tongue of the lion wash his face as it knocked him to the ground. Androclus opened his eyes—face-to-face with his friend from the forest. Instead of pouncing to kill, even after days of hunger and torment, the lion, once so gently cared for, fawned over the man like a friendly dog.[6]

The first words of Esther 6:1 are "During *that* night." They corre-spond to an earlier expression in the story, *"that* day" (Esther 5:9), when Haman went out from his first banquet with the king and queen, saw the unbending Mordecai, bragged to his friends and family, and decided to build the gallows right then and there. Without question, the author of Esther wants us to understand the ever-increasing speed at which events are taking place—a pace that seems to be out of the control of the characters in the story, and thus a speed that God alone can regulate.[7]

"During *that* night." While all of Susa slept, the king was restless. Of all the nights to suffer insomnia, this was the one. The king knew nothing of the plan to kill Mordecai. Haman would reveal it to him the next morning in order to get his approval for the execution. So while Haman slept, while Mordecai slept, while all of Susa—in fact, while all of Persia slept—the king couldn't. Something was disturbing him. He was restless. Perhaps he was wondering about the day's events and what Esther might have on her mind. Why did she break palace protocol and put her life on the line the way she did? Why the private banquet with Haman? In ancient times harems were a hotbed of political intrigue. Was there a coup in the making? Something going on between Esther and Haman or rival factions in the harem? Already one plot had been foiled against Ahasuerus (Esther 2:21-23), and 14 years later (464 B.C.) one of Ahasuerus's courtiers would assassinate him.[8] Assassination plots were not uncommon in palace politics. It's quite possible that Ahasuerus pulled out the "Book of Remembrances, the Chronicles"—the historical records of the kingdom—so he could reflect on what had been taking place around him lately. Perhaps he wanted to see who was doing what—see who was on his side or who might be shifting allegiance.

So Ahasuerus carefully listened through the night to the reading of the chronicles, his mind attentive to the record of Persia's history, hoping to find something, but probably wishing more that he was just imagining things and that the droning sound of the reading would bore him to sleep.

Suddenly, however, the recounting of the incident in which a man named Mordecai had uncovered a plot against him caught Ahasuerus's attention. "Stop! Wait a minute!" he told the reader. "What honor or dignity has been bestowed on Mordecai for this?" he asked (Esther 6:3).

"Nothing has been done for him," his attending servants replied.

98

"H'mm. Got to do something," he mused. It was an embarrassing oversight. During the Medo-Persian Era failure to extend honor to a deserving benefactor wasn't politically or socially correct.[9] Yet the king had done exactly that. God moves the heart of the king, who suddenly realizes that he owes his life and throne to an obscure Jew named Mordecai. A man who, up to this moment in time, meant nothing to him. Suddenly he's the king's top priority.

An In-Your-Face Assignment

As soon as Ahasuerus heard that Mordecai had received no reward, he began to imagine what he might do to reward the man for his great deed. Then he had to figure out who would help him carry it out. And so he asked the logical question: "Who is in the court?" (verse 4).

Now Haman had just entered the outer court of the king's palace in order to speak to the king about hanging Mordecai on the gallows. The sun was barely over the horizon and Haman had rushed to the palace as early as he could so he could hang Mordecai. "Let him come in," the king said (verse 5). So as Haman entered, Ahasuerus asked, "What is to be done for the man whom the king desires to honor?" (verse 6). The question caught Haman off guard. He had Mordecai on his mind right then, but honor was "his thing." It was no effort for him to shift gears to that topic. Suddenly we're inside his private inner world, listening to him say to himself, "Honor? Now, whom would the king desire to honor more than me? Yes . . . honor. Here's my chance to do it up right."

"For the man whom the king desires to honor, let them bring a royal robe which the king has worn, and the horse on which the king has ridden, and on whose head a royal crown has been placed; and let the robe and the horse be handed over to one of the king's most noble princes and let them array the man whom the king desires to honor and lead him on horseback through the city square, and proclaim before him, 'Thus it shall be done to the man whom the king desires to honor'" (verses 7-9).

Ahasuerus thought it was a great idea and said to Haman, "Take quickly the robes and the horse as you have said, and do so for Mordecai the Jew, who is sitting at the king's gate; do not fall short in anything of all that you have said" (verse 10). What Ahasuerus did not realize was that he, in essence, struck a hard blow to Haman's pride. The responsibility for holding the bridle of the horse on which an honored man rode was considered an honor in itself. Haman had himself asked that one of the king's "most noble princes" would carry out the assignment (verse 9). Ahasuerus would have properly assumed that Haman would feel honored to have the privilege of leading Mordecai throughout the city square. "Yet, for Haman, this honor is his shame."[10]

We can hear Haman thinking to himself, *Oh, man! This has got to be a mistake. The king couldn't possibly have said that hated name, could he? What's going on?* Talk about an in-your-face assignment! It had humiliation written all over it. "The words Haman had to proclaim must have been gravel in his mouth."[11] "So Haman took the robe and the horse, and arrayed Mordecai, and led him on horseback through the city square, and proclaimed before him, 'Thus it shall be done to the man whom the king desires to honor'" (verse 11).

"So Mordecai is elevated not upon the stake but upon a horse of honor and Haman cries out his honor before him. The one who would not bow down is now being acknowledged as honored by the one who demanded honor of him. A splendid role reversal which bodes ill in the eyes of all who know Haman. The last paragraph is full of the word *fall*."[12] When the bitter experience finally ended, "Haman hurried home, mourning, with his head covered. And Haman recounted to Zeresh his wife and all his friends everything that had happened to him. Then his wise men and Zeresh his wife said to him, 'If Mordecai, before whom you have begun to fall, is of Jewish origin, you will not overcome him, but will surely fall before him'" (verses 12, 13).

When our family visited England's infamous Tower of London, it intrigued me to learn about the bizarre Chapel of St. Peter in Chains that sits inside the walls of the grisly castle. The British had a curious way of doing things in those days. They would behead their political prisoners out on Tower Hill, and then bury their headless bodies under the flagstone tile of the Chapel of St. Peter in Chains. The rulers would stick the heads of the luckless men and women on a gibbet on the London Bridge for all to see and the birds to eat.

Through the years some 1,500 headless bodies were buried in the floor and under the altar of this infamous chapel. One gets an eerie feeling standing in that chapel, as if the place is haunted by a thousand injustices and ghoulish deaths. Suddenly Revelation's graphic imagery of souls under the altar crying out "How long, O Lord, holy and true, wilt Thou refrain from judging and avenging our blood?" finds poignant meaning (Rev. 6:9, 10).

Mordecai must have been the most surprised man in the kingdom. He had gone on living his life unnoticed, unrewarded, and unappreciated—until this pivotal day. I want you to catch how the king identifies Mordecai. He characterized Mordecai as "the Jew" (Esther 6:10). "Go honor Mordecai the Jew," he ordered. Providentially, on the lips of a pagan king, God is beginning to affirm both His people and His truth. Even Haman's wise men and Zeresh his wife catch the implication. "If Mordecai, before whom you have begun to fall, is of Jewish origin, you will not overcome him, but will surely fall before him" (verse 13). How did they know? How could they be so certain? What was there about being Jewish and winning? No doubt a host of stories of God's mighty acts of deliverance circulated among the people. God's promise of turning the moral/spiritual/justice pineapple cake right side up was also well known. In the sudden turn of events, the incredible reversals already taking place, they sensed God was beginning to act on behalf of His people once more. And they were right.

Sometimes faithfulness to God goes unnoticed, unrewarded, and unappreciated. And so with truth. It is often on the scaffold. *How long?* we wonder to ourselves. But when no one seems to notice, God does. The story of Mordecai is the account of a gracious God who will cause both His people and His truth to be honored in the appropriate time, at the most profound moment. And ultimately, for eternity.

Ellen White tells us that "the reverence of God's people for His law is a constant rebuke to those who have cast off the fear of the Lord. . . . Today, as in the days of Esther and Mordecai, the Lord will vindicate His truth and His people."[13] Revelation promises a moment during the moral and spiritual darkness of the crisis in the end-time—when it appears that truth and the faithful people of God will be completely overwhelmed—that a mighty angel will come down from heaven having great authority and lighting the earth with his glory (Rev. 18:1). It will be a marvelous moment of compelling reversal as the call resounds throughout a world of darkness, "Come out of her, my people, that you may not participate in her sins and that you may not receive of her plagues; for her sins have piled up as high as heaven, and God has remembered her iniquities" (verses 4, 5). Soon afterward a chorus of amazed voices will resound through the heavens, "Hallelujah! Salvation and glory and power belong to God; because His judgments are true and righteous, for He has judged the great harlot who was corrupting the earth with her immorality, and He has avenged the blood of His bondservants on her" (Rev. 19:1, 2). It won't be only angels who sing such things. Every human being who is on the right side of this grand reversal will likewise shout for joy. Daniel says it best: "Those who have insight will shine brightly like the brightness of the expanse of heaven, and those who lead the many to righteousness, like the stars forever and ever" (Dan. 12:3). Many things already taking place in our world today affirm this biblical teaching of surprise reversal when God will honor His people and His truth at the most propitious moment.

Returning to Esther's day, we can be sure that everyone in Susa had been watching and were wondering about what had just taken place. After all, they had been astir with horror and confusion following Haman's edict for ethnic cleansing (Esther 3:15). Certainly, by now everyone knew Mordecai was a Jew. So what was this all about? Mordecai the Jew being led around in honor at the hand of Prime Minister Haman, who had himself concocted the plan for exterminating Jews? It was an incongruous procession. George Dickinson puts it this way: "When it was over, Mordecai returned to the gate and took up his usual duties, as though the whole thing had been part of the day's work. But his fellow officers didn't take it that way. The king had honored an erstwhile outcast. Now respect and deference were showered on him obsequiously by the same lips that had poured contempt on him and his people only hours before. The incident quickly became a citywide topic of discussion. What would now happen to Mordecai the Jew, and all the other Jews?"[14] At a later moment, we're told, those same people in Susa burst out in shouting and rejoicing. Why? The upside-down cake had finally been turned right side up.

At some point God will honor His people and His truth. When He does, a watching world will take note. So the Lord now calls us to faithfulness, waiting, and—at times—patient endurance (Rev. 14:12; 13:10). "God is not unjust so as to forget your work and the love which you have shown toward His name, in having ministered and in still ministering to the saints" (Heb. 6:10). "Thanks be to God, who gives us the victory through our Lord Jesus Christ. Therefore, my beloved brethren, be steadfast, immovable, always abounding in the work of the Lord, knowing that your toil is not in vain in the Lord" (1 Cor. 15:57, 58). "And let us not grow weary while doing good, for in due season we shall reap if we do not lose heart" (Gal. 6:9, NKJV).

Like King Ahasuerus, God, too, has His book of remembrance, His chronicles that He will read and respond to, not out of forgetfulness, but sovereign providence: "Then those who feared the Lord spoke to one another, and the Lord gave attention and heard it, and a book of remembrance was written before Him for those who fear the Lord and who esteem His name. 'And they will be Mine,' says the Lord of hosts, 'on the day that I prepare My own possession, and I will spare them as a man spares his own son who serves him.' So you will again distinguish between the righteous and the wicked, between one who serves God and one who does not serve Him" (Mal. 3:16-18).

"Not one cloud has fallen upon the church that God has not prepared for; not one opposing force has risen to counterwork the work of God but He has foreseen. . . . *Truth is inspired and guarded by God; it will live, and will succeed, although it may appear at times to be overshadowed.* The gospel of Christ is the law exemplified in character. *The deceptions practiced against it, every device vindicating falsehood, every error forged by satanic agencies, will eventually be eternally broken, and the triumph of truth will be like the appearing of the sun at noonday.*"[15]

"The great work of the gospel is not to close with less manifestation of the power of God than marked its opening," Ellen White tells us.[16] "The message will be carried not so much by argument as by the deep conviction of the Spirit of God. The arguments have been presented. The seed has been sown, and now it will spring up and bear fruit. The publications distributed by missionary workers have exerted their influence, yet many whose minds were impressed have been prevented from fully comprehending the truth or from yielding obedience. *Now the rays of light penetrate everywhere, the truth is seen in its clearness,* and the honest children of God sever the bands which have held them. Family connections, church relations, are powerless to stay them now. Truth is more precious than all besides. Notwithstanding the agencies combined against the truth, a large number take their stand upon the Lord's side."[17]

It will be a grand moment of reversal. Such dramatic honor is the only kind that God bestows.

Any Heart Is Like Water

Esther 6 is filled with incredible irony and astonishing reversal. As we've seen, it's all about honor and dishonor. But more important, it is about God's providential work. Up till this moment in the story God has been *behind the seen* in a rather obscure way. No one knows for sure where He is or what He has in mind for His endangered people. But now unexpected and dramatic events begin to take place that tell us that God has not been out of touch or passive. He has not forgotten His people or His promises to them. In fact, He is orchestrating events. Just look at a few of the more significant coincidences that occur in the 14 verses of chapter 6:

> ➤ The timing of the events is such that they occur the same night that Haman is building a gallows on which to hang Mordecai (Esther 6:1; 5:14);

> ➤ The king's inability to sleep (Esther 6:1);

> ➤ The king's decision to read the chronicles rather than to find some other means by which either to amuse himself or to lull himself to sleep (verse 1);

> ➤ The reading of the specific story about Mordecai's actions that avoided a palace coup and the discovery that he had never been rewarded (verses 2, 3);

> ➤ Haman's eagerness to hang Mordecai that drives the prime minister to be at the king's courtyard early in the morning (verse 4);

➤ Haman being identified as the only one in the courtyard at the time (verse 5);

➤ Haman's misinterpretation of the king's question (verse 6);

➤ Haman being required to honor the man whom he most hates, Mordecai the Jew (verses 10, 11);

➤ The servant's arrival when Haman is at his lowest to hasten him to the queen's banquet, where he will fall even lower (verse 14).

Such apparent coincidences interject the reality that God is working all things for good in the end. The author of Esther wants us to recognize that the Lord alone rescues Mordecai and that the man has not had any hand whatsoever in his own deliverance.[18] Furthermore, he leads us to see how "God works providentially through even the day-to-day circumstances of life. He works through such human events as insomnia, the reading of a specific text of a specific book, the anger of a man, the timing of events, the words of unbelievers, and the actions of people doing their jobs. Nothing in life is too small or insignificant for God to oversee or use to ensure the good of his people or the downfall of his enemies."[19] Each "coincidence" points to God's awesome sovereign power.

Proverbs tells us that "the king's heart is like channels of water in the hand of the Lord; He turns it wherever He wishes" (Prov. 21:1). So it was with mighty King Ahasuerus. In the end God's will prevailed.

God can handle anyone and anything. He can transform your husband, wife, or kids. The Lord can deal with the person who gives you grief, your ex-mate, that person who made you all those promises and broke most of them. And He can even handle your enemy. In fact, He can work out the most intimidating situation, because in the hand of the Lord, any heart is like water.[20] You can trust Him to preserve the honor of His people and the honor of His truth as well.

One of the twentieth century's best-sellers was Henri Charrière's *Papillon*, the story of his daring escape from Devil's Island. Charrière was just 25 years old when France convicted him for a murder he had not committed and sentenced him to life imprisonment in the penal colony of French Guinea. A tattoo of a butterfly on his chest earned him the nickname of "Papillon" (French for butterfly). One thought obsessed him: escape. Forty-two days after his arrival on the island, he made his first break, traveling 1,500 miles on the open sea in a tiny boat. But when the authorities captured him, they sent him to solitary confinement on the infamous Devil's Island. No one had ever escaped from this prison until Papillon did it by flinging himself into the boiling sea with a makeshift raft made of two bags of coconuts. Eventually he found sanctuary in Venezuela, where he received citizenship and authored his unbelievable story.

Charrière had not made his escape alone. Chang, an old Chinese professional pirate had helped him plan the escape and gave advice on what to do and who to look up when he reached the mainland. "Be careful," Chang cautioned. "When you almost mainland, there's quicksand. Never walk on quicksand; it suck you up. Wait next tide to push you in bush so you grab branches. If not, you finished." Sylvain, a big athletic guy, joined him in the escape.

On a full moonlit night Charrière and Sylvain plunged into a temporary pool formed by incoming waves among the craggy rocks along the jagged coastline. One had to leap just as the pool filled to avoid smacking into the rocks. Within moments the waves carried them out to sea on their makeshift rafts. Two days later the current had swung them by the mainland. The shore was near now, and the waves raced toward it in long straight lines. They could see the trees along the shoreline and branches awash in the sea. Above the noise of the breakers came the shrieks of thousands of wading birds. A little farther, then *ploof.* Charrière had run aground in the quicksand. It was low tide. It would be hours before the rising tide could bring him closer to the bushes.

Sylvain was about 100 yards on Charrière's right. He began making motions as if trying to shout something. What was the stupid ox doing? He was leaving his raft! Had he lost his mind? If he started walking, he'd sink in deeper with each step. Charrière tried to whistle, but his mouth was too dry. The poor guy who got stuck in that quicksand was done for.

Sylvain kept making signs Charrière couldn't understand. Suddenly he realized that Sylvain was already being sucked in. The sound of the wail reached him. Charrière lay down flat on his raft, dug his hands into

the quicksand, and pulled with all his might. The raft crept forward perhaps 20 yards. He could see Sylvain now, 10 yards from his raft, buried
up to his waist. "Sylvain! Try to lie flat on your raft! Try to free your
legs!" he yelled. Again Charrière clawed furiously at the sand. Rage
gave him tremendous strength, and he moved another 30 yards. By now
an hour had passed, and Sylvain was up to his chest in quicksand. The
tide began to rise. Soon the other man was up to his armpits.

As Charrière writes, Sylvain's "eyes [were] wide open and glued
to mine. I wanted only not to lose those staring eyes. . . . He knew
he was dying there in the muck, three hundred yards from the
promised land. I lay down again and went back to clawing at the sand,
which was almost liquid now. Our eyes stayed riveted on each other.
. . . Another giant breaker covered me with an avalanche of water and
I floated my raft five or six yards forward. When the breaker had
passed on, I looked up. Sylvain was gone. The quicksand was covered
with a thin layer of foamy water. Suddenly I was seized with a shame-
ful animal reaction: the instinct for survival swept all sentiment away.
I said to myself, You may still be alive. But when you're in the bush
alone, without a friend, your cavale [escape] will be in trouble. A
roller broke over my back—I was sitting now—and brought me back
to reality. . . . For several minutes I couldn't get my breath. The raft
slid forward another few yards, and it was only then . . . that I wept
for my friend: We were so near. If only you hadn't gotten off! . . .
Why did you do it? . . . Too much sun? . . . Did you lose the strength
to endure . . . ? Why couldn't a man like you take the punishment for
a few more hours? The breakers kept on rolling in, . . . but I determined not to budge from my raft until I had a branch . . . in my hand.
Twenty yards to go. It must have been another hour before the last
wave literally hurled me into the trees."[21]

Just three hundred yards from the promised land. If only Sylvain
hadn't gotten off. Why did he do it? Sometimes we lose the strength
to endure. In the midst of injustice or obscurity our unsung faithfulness to God seems to be taking us nowhere. *How long?* we wonder
to ourselves. *Does it even make a difference?* But the promise of Esther
is that a gracious God will cause both you and His truth to be hon-

ored in the appropriate time and for eternity. He's *behind the seen* right now working for you. Just stay on the raft. He'll see you through to freedom.

---

[1] "Toads and Diamonds," *The Riverside Anthology of Children's Literature,* ed. Judith Saltman (Dallas: Houghton-Mifflin Company, 1985), pp. 292, 293.

[2] M. V. Fox, *Character and Ideology in the Book of Esther,* p. 178.

[3] *Ibid.,* pp. 179, 180.

[4] *Ibid.,* p. 180.

[5] Johanna W. H. Bos, *Ruth, Esther, Jonah* (Atlanta: John Knox Press, 1986), p. 60.

[6] Alice Gray, *More Stories for the Heart* (Sisters, Oreg.: Multnomah Publishers, 1997), pp. 104-106; William J. Bennett, *The Book of Virtues* (New York: Simon & Schuster, 1993), pp. 118, 119.

[7] A. B. Luter and B. C. Davis, *God Behind the Seen,* p. 266.

[8] "Ahasuerus," *Nelson's Illustrated Bible Dictionary.*

[9] Luter and Davis, pp. 267, 268.

[10] *Ibid.,* p. 273.

[11] J. G. Baldwin, *Esther,* p. 90.

[12] Bos, p. 62.

[13] E. G. White, *Prophets and Kings,* pp. 605, 606.

[14] George T. Dickinson, *Hidden Patterns and the Grand Design* (Washington, D.C.: Review and Herald Pub. Assn., 1967), p. 98.

[15] Ellen G. White, *Selected Messages* (Washington, D.C.: Review and Herald Pub. Assn., 1958), book 2, p. 108. (Italics supplied.)

[16] ——— , *The Great Controversy* (Mountain View, Calif.: Pacific Press Pub. Assn., 1911), p. 611.

[17] *Ibid.,* p. 612. (Italics supplied.)

[18] Luter and Davis, p. 278.

[19] *Ibid.*

[20] C. R. Swindoll, *Esther: A Woman of Strength and Dignity,* p. 100.

[21] Henri Charrière, *Papillon* (New York: William Morrow and Company, 1970), pp. 379, 380.

CHAPTER EIGHT

WHEN THE END JUSTIFIES THE BEAMS

Esther 7:1-10

In November of 1998 Iraq taught the world how to put the most powerful military in history on a leash. With just 15 minutes to go before cruise missiles would leap from their launchpads and with attack aircraft already in the air, President Clinton canceled the long-threatened air strikes. He claimed that Saddam Hussein had backed down. The Iraqis, though, boasted that they had once again pulled the diplomatic rug out from underneath the United States. While it appears that the Iraqis got wind of the coming onslaught just moments before it was too late and scrambled at the last minute to avert it, they did succeed in essentially neutralizing the $250 billion-a-year military of the United States. Analysts assert that the Iraqis won the first round through two forms of strategy—asymmetrical warfare and information warfare.

Asymmetrical warfare takes place when a weaker enemy manages to render his stronger opponent's advantages meaningless by coming up with an innovative strategy. For the Iraqis, that meant moving their valuable assets into high-population areas, where civilians would die if attacked. They gambled that Clinton would be anxious to avoid world reaction to the 10,000 Iraqi casualties predicted by the Pentagon.

Information warfare deals with perceptions and who creates reality. Facts are irrelevant—image and repetition are everything. For Iraqis, that meant endless broadcasting of video footage of hungry Iraqi children, Baghdad hospitals without medicine, and civilians forced to sell their last possessions to survive.

Through these two forms of strategy Iraq once again convinced America's leadership that political defeat would be the price of military victory. And so we blinked.[1] Analysts tell us that blink cost the U.S. $1 billion!

Esther may have never heard of "asymmetrical" or "information" warfare, but going up against a formidable foe such as Haman—the prime minister, the major shaker and mover in the Persian Empire second only to the king, a man of incredible wealth, a shrewd master of political intrigue, one who already had the signed edict in his hand for the extermination of the Jew—called for a strategy that would render all his apparent advantages meaningless. She needed a strategy that would place everything Haman had planned and signed into policy in a new and different light. Somehow she must control both the way the critical issues would be discussed and the flow of information. Timing was crucial, as well as the choice of words and the image of reality her strategy would create. The queen was at a disadvantage, the underdog. Only "asymmetrical" and "information" warfare were available in her arsenal—except of course her behind-the-seen God to whom she had surrendered herself to be used and guided.

It was a high-stakes moment. Esther must prepare the king for the revelation of Haman's real nature, then show the prime minister for what he really was. The situation was a very ticklish matter. Haman was the king's trusted right-hand man and a drinking buddy to boot (Esther 3:15). Revealing the perfidy and treachery of some trusted friend is always a delicate thing—which is why Esther moved slowly.[2] "Haman's slimy guise of friendship must be stripped from him in the presence of the king."[3] Nothing can be done to deliver the kingdom from the evil influence of Haman until the king clearly sees Haman's true character.[4]

Now the occasion for that revelation of evil has come. It's a moment of suspense and sinister possibilities. The collision course between Mordecai and Haman approaches a climax, and Esther finds herself caught in the middle. I've often wondered how Hollywood would handle this high adrenaline moment of exposing the sinister to the vulnerable unsuspecting. It was a high-suspense showdown for allegiance, or at least the upper hand. All the ingredients are here for a gripping R-rated movie—extravagant wealth and a drunken orgy (chap. 1); gorgeous women and sexually explicit scenes (chap. 2); grisly violence (chap. 9); and an unfurling drama of who will succeed in the high-stakes propaganda game of creating reality and controlling destiny. The book of Esther has it all! Scripture is so honest. Could the controversy between Christ and Satan be made more vivid? Or the part we ourselves play in the incessant epic?

"Now the king and Haman came to drink wine with Esther the queen" (Esther 7:1). I can imagine the three of them sipping fine royal wine together from some of those golden goblets we learned about in chapter 1. It's a superb moment of sensory ambiance as candles flicker, aromas tantalize, and the tingle of alcohol combines with exquisite taste. Halfway through the sumptuous meal the king gets down to the subject that had become a compelling curiosity in his mind. "What's on your mind, Queen Esther? I'll give it to you" (see verse 2). Charmed by her graciousness and fascinated by the splendor of her table, he repeats the extravagant promise he has given twice before: "Just tell me what it is, and it will be done—even to half of the kingdom."

"At this fleeting moment the eyes of Ahasuerus waited expectantly, little aware of the thunderclap soon to rock the room. Looking at Esther, he saw nothing but loveliness. Gazing at the table, the equal of which he had rarely seen for taste and elegance, he thought of the unusual setting of this whole thing and wondered what his queen was up to."[5]

Across the table was another set of eyes, cunning and cruel, that waited as well to hear the queen's request. One wonders if for a moment Esther gazed piercingly into Haman's unsuspecting eyes. Certainly she knew that she must deal with the man who possessed them as one would a deadly snake.

Did Esther's heart pound in her throat as she realized her very life and her nation's future hung in the balance of the next few words she would speak and the response of her husband, the king? Every word she speaks now is decisive. They will make the difference between life or death. The King waits. Haman waits. The silence is excruciating. She's not quite sure just what to say or what will happen next. But the king has once again opened the door for Esther. He has made it easy for her to share what's disturbing her. For the third time Ahasuerus invites her with gentle words of promise: "Esther, what's on your heart? Tell me, and I will give it to you, up to half of my kingdom." In that moment of opportunity Esther takes courage and presses her request.

Now she wastes no more time or beats around the bush: "If I have found favor in your sight, O king, and if it please the king," she begins (in other words, "If you love me"), "let my life be given me as my petition, and my people as my request" (verse 3). Without doubt she spoke with drama and passion. What she said startled the king. Esther's life in danger? How? Haman likely began to read in the fire of her flashing eyes the disquieting harbinger of something ominous.

"We have been sold," she exclaimed. "I and my people, to be destroyed, to be killed and to be annihilated" (verse 4). The astonishment of the king increases. Destroyed? Killed? Annihilated? They are the very same words Haman used in his extermination edict against the Jews (Esther 3:13). Haman catches the similarities and squirms in his seat, the reality dawning on him that he just may be getting caught in his own trap.

"If we had only been sold as slaves," Esther continues, "I would have remained silent, for then our plight would not be such as to injure the king's interests" (Esther 7:4, paraphrase). Another careful choice of words. Surprisingly, Esther employs the very same word that Haman used when he first proposed his pogrom against the Jews. The little word *shavah* does not appear frequently in the Hebrew Scriptures, but it means "for one's best interests." When Haman first spoke to the king about the Jews, he boldly asserted, "This is a scattered people. This is a people who have their own laws. This is a people who do not obey the king. It is not in the king's best interest to keep these people around" (see Esther 3:8).

Esther gambles too, and appeals for what she thinks will cause her husband to join her side. "My life is not the issue," she says, "not even those of my people. Rather my request is for what is in the best interest of the kingdom. What is best for you." By implication, whoever is against her and her people is also against the king.[6]

So Haman and Esther both appealed to what they hoped the king would consider as being to his own advantage. "It is not in the king's best interest to keep these people around," Haman had claimed. "You've promised me half of the kingdom, but all I want is what is best for you and your kingdom," Esther in her turn would now have the king believe.[7]

112

The familiar words ring in the king's ear now with a different contextual nuance than when Haman first used them. Suddenly they have a different meaning. The choice of words, the flow of information, the context in which it is communicated, begins to frame a different kind of reality than what Haman had created. Knowing he had not deliberately devised a law to destroy his lovely queen, Ahasuerus asks with indignation, "Who is he? Where is he? Who would presume to do something like this?" (see Esther 7:5). I can imagine another incredible moment of silence that left Haman dismayed and utterly confused. Esther's heart pounds louder, her mouth dries. An adrenaline rush skyrockets the king's blood pressure.

Realizing that her moment has arrived, Esther neither stammers nor hesitates. Leveling her gaze at Haman and likely pointing her finger at him across the room, she speaks in firm measured tones: "A foe and an enemy, is this wicked Haman!" (verse 6). Esther not only identifies Haman as the villain; she also characterizes him, giving him a sinister face. "A foe, an enemy, this wicked Haman!" Esther could have answered straightforwardly in a sheepish half-whispered matter-of-fact way: "It's Haman. Your prime minister." But no, she knows how the king thinks, his moods. She understands what he is capable of doing when he's mad. It is now when his blood is boiling—now when his indignation is white-hot—that she should embellish the facts with emotion and dramatic imagery. Esther is shrewd enough to say what needs to be said now that Haman's mask is beginning to fall.[8] "A foe, an enemy, this wicked Haman!"

As Esther has put the case, Haman is a traitor to the king as well as an enemy of the Jews. Her words open the king's eyes. He had had no idea of Esther's nationality. Nor had he suspected anything of Haman's sinister character. For Haman, the realization that he had inadvertently threatened the queen's life was a knockout blow on top of his earlier humiliation of having to lead Mordecai around the city wearing the king's robe and riding the king's horse while proclaiming, "Thus it shall be done to the man whom the king desires to honor."[9] As Haman now cringes in abject terror, "Ahasuerus rises, furious with wrath and indignation. He has been duped by this man, who has sought to further his own ends by inveigling the king into signing the death decree. Now he sees Haman in his true light. Going into the palace garden, the king, boiling with anger, wonders how this wicked scheme was put over on him. How could he have been so blind? Why had he tolerated a prime minister so bent on ruining some of his best subjects? Esther among them! And faithful Mordecai, who had saved his life!"[10]

In the meantime Haman "stayed to beg for his life from Queen Esther, for he saw that harm had been determined against him by the king" (verse 7). How ironic that the once-powerful Haman, the enemy of the Jews, now pleads for his very life from not only a Jew, but a woman as well. O how the proud have fallen and the tables turned.

We'll never know how long Ahasuerus fumed in the palace garden, but at the very moment he stepped back into Esther's private banquet room, Haman is in the act of falling on the couch where Esther reclined (verse 8). The form of the Hebrew verb implies he is "in motion." Haman is somewhere between standing upright and lying on Queen Esther's couch.[11] His posture only made matters worse. "To approach the couch upon which Esther reclined was a breach of palace etiquette, but to fall upon her couch or to touch her was an affront to the king himself—perhaps even an act of treason."[12] "Will he even assault the queen with me in the house?" Ahasuerus wonders out loud (verse 8). By his improper act, Haman now solidly seals his own death sentence. The covering of his face indicates his condemnation to death (verse 8).

Thus sinister Haman reveals himself to be a mere fool. Everything he does in the story "is manifestly foolish, as he is buffeted about and driven by his passions and impulses. His anger makes him unable to wait for his revenge and leads him to push fate and try to kill Mordecai prematurely. The consequence is that he erects the instrument of his own death and rushes straight to humiliation. His fatuous assumption that he alone is worthy of the king's honors makes a public fool out of him. He, the vizier and high nobleman, has to conduct his enemy on horseback as his herald through the city square, all this exacerbated to the extreme by the fact that his conflict with Mordecai is well known among the palace officials who are watching the display. His folly finally unmasks itself in his rash fall on Esther's couch, an act which is the immediate cause of his death. Haman is a buffoon, a clever fool. . . . Haman would not be bothered by being shown to be deeply evil, but he would be mortified to be revealed as an impulsive bungler."[13] Such is the self-defeating nature of evil.[14]

At this point Harbonah, one of the king's eunuchs, decides to become a tattletale. Maybe Harbonah liked Mordecai. Perhaps Haman's haughtiness disgusted him. Or he was just an opportunist. Whatever! Although the king had not asked him for any advice, Harbonah reads the moment well and openly "declares to anyone who might be in earshot in an offhanded fashion that a gallows exists—a seventy-five-foot-high gallows that is close at hand, in fact, at Haman's house."[15] As he points through the door or window to the nearly eight-story-high gibbet Haman had constructed during the night, he quips, "Behold . . . the gallows . . . Haman made for Mordecai who spoke good on behalf of the king!" (verse 9). That's all that it took. *Great idea!* the king thought as he looked out and saw the gallows towering above the city. "Hang him on it" (verse 9). That's it! They impaled Haman on the very gallows that he had prepared for Mordecai. The end justified the beams! Or shall we say, Haman finally got the point!

A Real Eye-opener

The seventh chapter of the book of Esther is a spine-tingling, unmasking scene.[16] It was high drama. The first-time reader does not know where the plot is heading until the very last verse. It seems as if nothing can be done to deliver God's people from the sinister influence of Haman until the king recognizes Haman's true character.[17] "Haman's slimy guise of friendship must be stripped from him in the presence of the king."[18] Evil must be shown for what it really is.

When we remember Esther's future orientation—the paradigm it projects with respect to the end-time struggle between good and evil—we can sense the larger message in this grand unmasking scene and gain incredible insights into the great controversy between good and evil in the last days. Before the end, God will expose evil for what it really is. The whole world will see its true nature. "The trying experiences that came to God's people in the days of Esther were not peculiar to that age alone. The revelator, looking down the ages to the close of time, has declared, 'The dragon was wroth with the woman, and went to make war with the remnant of her seed, which keep the commandments of God, and have the testimony of Jesus Christ' (Rev. 12:17, KJV). . . . The decree that will finally go forth against the remnant people of God will be very similar to that issued by Ahasuerus against the Jews. Today the enemies of the true church see in the little company keeping the Sabbath commandment, a Mordecai at the gate. The reverence of God's people for His law is a constant rebuke to those who have cast off the fear of the Lord and are trampling on His Sabbath. . . . Today, as in the days of Esther and Mordecai, the Lord will vindicate His truth and His people." [19] While the deliverance for Esther and her people was local and only temporary, it foreshadowed the great rescue of God's people that would appear in the future. [20]

Just as God's truth and God's people will in time be honored—vindicated before a watching world, as we have learned in the previous chapter—so will evil stand fully unmasked in front of a surprised world before the return of Jesus. In the last days, as the final climax reaches full heat, two things will take place almost simultaneously—God's truth and God's people will receive honor, on the one hand; evil and falsehood are unmasked and shown to be the sinister poison they really are, on the other hand. God will do nothing to deliver our world from evil, nothing to rescue His people from this world of evil, until our world recognizes evil's true sinister character. In the end, neither we nor the world will remain in doubt as to the issues that will be fought in the last great struggle between Christ and Satan. Not surprisingly, the people of God will unmask the enemy.

The Great Controversy has a chapter titled "The Final Warning." It refers to the mighty angel of Revelation 18—the angel who comes down from heaven with great authority and proclaims, "Fallen, fallen is Babylon the great! And she has become a dwelling place of demons and a prison of every unclean spirit, and a prison of every unclean and hateful bird. For all the nations have drunk of the wine of the passion of her immorality, and the kings of the earth have committed acts of immorality with her, and the merchants of the earth have become rich by the wealth of her sensuality" (Rev. 18:1-4). A gracious voice from heaven then declares, "Come out of her, my people" (verse 5). Ellen White comments that "God still has a people in Babylon; and before the visitation of His judgments these faithful ones must be called out, that they partake not of her sins and 'receive not of her plagues.' Hence the movement symbolized by the angel coming down from heaven, lightening the earth with his glory and crying mightily with a strong voice, announcing the sins of Babylon. In connection with his message the call is heard: 'Come out of her, my people.' These announcements, uniting with the third angel's message, constitute the final warning to be given to the inhabitants of the earth."[21]

"There are many who have never had an opportunity to hear the special truths for this time. . . . He who reads every heart and tries every motive will leave none who desire a knowledge of the truth, to be deceived as to the issues of the controversy. The decree [observance of the false Sabbath on pain of death] is not to be urged upon the people blindly. Everyone is to have sufficient light to make his decision intelligently."[22]

As Esther did to unmask Haman, so "the Lord will work through humble instruments, leading the minds of those who consecrate themselves to His service. . . . Men of faith and prayer will be constrained to go forth with holy zeal, declaring the words which God gives them. *The sins of Babylon will be laid open.* The fearful results of enforcing observance of the church by civil authority, the inroads of spiritualism, the stealthy but rapid progress of the papal power—*all will be unmasked.* By these solemn warnings the people will be stirred. Thousands upon thousands will listen who have never heard words like these. In amazement they hear the testimony that Babylon is the church, fallen because of her errors and sins, because of her rejection of the truth sent to her from heaven."[23]

What a glorious moment that will be!

As with Esther, it will be high drama, heart-stopping reality, and no easy experience. And yet, "the rays of light [will] penetrate everywhere, the truth is seen in its clearness, and the honest children of God sever the bands which have held them. Family connections, church relations, are powerless to stay them now. Truth is more precious than all besides. Notwithstanding the agencies combined against the truth, a large number take their stand upon the Lord's side."[24]

Again, what a glorious moment for God that will be!

Scripture's last book promises a dramatic unmasking of evil. Revelation tells us it will come quickly—in a mere hour according to prophetic imagery (Rev. 18:17). Babylon's supportive Euphrates waters will dry up forever, opening the way for her quick and complete destruction by the approaching kings of the east and their glorious leader riding on the white horse (Rev. 16:12; Rev. 19:11–16). By that time the peoples and multitudes and nations and tongues that these waters symbolize (Rev. 17:15) will have either withdrawn their support of or their participation in mystic Babylon's evil (Rev. 17:16; 18:4). Some will have even turned upon her, stripping her naked, and burning her with fire, as in ancient days when they hurled judgment upon an adulterous wife of a priest (Rev. 17:16).

When you read the book of Esther, Ahasuerus is in the dark throughout and doesn't know what's really going on around him. He has no grasp for the moral/spiritual implications of all that's taking place. The Persian ruler understands neither who Haman is nor what he is up to. Ahasuerus needs help putting things together—in understanding the moral, spiritual, and even political implications of decisions, events, and personalities. Someone must help him to see that Haman is evil and an enemy and that Mordecai (the Jew) really has the king's best interest at heart. That the people of God are there for his good and for the good of the kingdom. It is no small detail that the book of Esther ends with Mordecai as one "who sought the good of his people and one who spoke for the welfare of his whole nation" (Esther 10:3). Haman is treacherous, seeking to destroy, kill, annihilate. In contrast, Mordecai preserves lives, speaks peace, and has the welfare of all at heart. And so Esther must unmask evil in the eyes of the king. And it is for him to realize the blessings that God's people alone can bring to both him and the world.

As the dramatic suspense-filled events unraveled before their eyes, the watching Gentile population of the Persian Empire likewise began to see things in an entirely new light. Many of them, too, had been dismayed by Haman's decree and the implications of his religio-ethnic plan of genocide (Esther 3:15). It was a dark troubling experience for those who longed for a world in which truth and peace and righteousness reigned. When the events in the ensuing drama began to turn in favor of God's people, "the city of Susa shouted and rejoiced" (Esther 8:15). Among God's people (the Jews) "there was light and gladness and joy and honor" (verse 16). In the process, a reverent awe filled many hearts, the fear of the Jews came upon them and "many among the peoples of the land became Jews" (verse 17). That tells us that as evil is unmasked in the final hours before probation closes, and the events take place that God in His sovereign providence has ordained, many will turn to the Lord and believe as in the days of Esther. They will leave the ranks of Satan and join with those under the blood-stained banner of Jesus Christ.

The bottom line, however, is that, as with Esther, the people of God—you and I—have a part to play in the apocalyptic unmasking of evil. When we read this chapter, we find that God's people will expose evil. God doesn't unmask it apart from the voice or actions of His people. Angels don't come down like Lone Rangers and dismantle evil, either. The people of God always play a prominent, active role in the process—with voice, influence, some clear action, or obedience.

As we have already learned, whenever we take a stand for what is right against the pressures of evil, it alters the course of history.[25] Our actions can free the unseen God to work His marvelous sovereign will. Had Esther refused to go before the king with the truth of the matter—had she kept quiet on the implications of Haman's sinister plan—she and her family would have undoubtedly perished, as Mordecai promised (Esther 4:14). But Esther chose to get involved, and because she did, God worked through her in a surprisingly powerful way. Through her He exposed Haman's sinister plot. Even now God works to unmask evil through His people. It will be even more so in the crisis at the end. God's people are the channels through which He works to illumine the minds of "those who sit in darkness and the shadow of death" (Luke 1:79).

Personal Moments of Truth

We need to grasp the deeper personal implications about this matter of involvement on the part of God's people. Not only do His people unmask evil, they can do so only as they have renewed their relationship with God. Here is the underlying message of Esther. The people of God in Esther's time were a compromising group living in exile. Like other Jews of the Exile, Esther and Mordecai were lukewarm Laodicean people. They were living in the world as if the world were all there was. But as God awakened them to the solemn life-and-death issues of their time and they spent time in prayer, rebuilding their faith and focusing their vision once more on God and His will, they received new spiritual power. Mordecai could take a stand for truth where he once had been compromising. Esther could now go forward to unmask Haman and his sinister plot. Her people could powerfully resist the onslaughts of those seeking to destroy them (Esther 9). Together, Esther, Mordecai, and the praying Jewish community exuded a profound spiritual influence that turned Gentile hearts to the living God.

But it all happened because God's people had first unmasked evil on a personal level. Personal insight preceded global insight. They could expose evil in their world because the Holy Spirit had first uncovered it in their own hearts. We cannot be part of God's work of spreading light until it has first shone brightly in our own private world. The Hamans within must be disclosed for what they really are. Then we must be bold enough to hang them on the gibbet and put them to death. That is the sentence that brings spiritual victory through God's grace. It must happen every time a Haman arises in our heart. "Lay aside the old self, which is being corrupted in accordance with the lusts of deceit, and . . . be renewed in the spirit of your mind, and put on the new self," says the apostle Paul (Eph. 4:22-24). "I have been crucified with Christ; and it is no longer I who live, but Christ lives in me" (Gal. 2:20).

Some of us get uneasy with any idea of unmasking the true status of our own hearts. Our human nature naturally resists religious/moral light piercing deep within. We draw back at the idea of any kind of judgment against our chosen way of life. Jesus spoke of hearts attracted to light and hearts afraid of light. "This is the judgment," He says, "that the light is come into the world, and men loved the darkness rather than the light; for their deeds were evil. For everyone who does evil hates the light, and does not come to the light, lest his deeds should be exposed. But he who practices the truth comes to the light, that his deeds may be manifested as having been wrought in God" (John 3:19-21).

Psalm 139 tells us that no matter where we go, God is there. Even when we try to hide in the darkness, He's there. It is not impenetrable to God. To Him, the night is as bright as the day. "Darkness and light are alike to Thee," Scripture asserts (Ps. 139:12). So, says David, "search me, O God, and know my heart; try me and know my anxious thoughts; and see if there be any hurtful way in me" (verses 22, 23).

Such moments of truth come when we suddenly catch a glimpse of the way we look to others and are horrified by what we see. God opens our eyes to see that the evil attitude or behavior or desire we have been treating as a friend—defending, protecting, building little fences about, making excuses for—is not our friend at all and never has been. It is in fact the bitterest enemy we have.[26] And it must be sentenced to death and hanged on the gallows if God is ever to use us to bring light to our hell-bound world.

The Society of Biblical Literature holds an annual convention that brings together Bible scholars from around the world to hear scholarly papers on literally hundreds of biblical, theological, and religious topics. Thousands usually attend these four-day-long meetings in a large convention center that can accommodate a multitude of simultaneous presentations, large plenary sessions, engaging scholarly dialogue, an enormous book display, energizing fellowship, and comfortable lodging.

The 1998 SBL meetings took place at Orlando's spectacular Walt Disney World Dolphin and Swan hotels. One of its highlights was "Revelation Live: A Dramatic Performance of the Apocalypse of John." Several hundred jammed into one of the large, elegant Swan ballrooms to hear New Testament scholar David Rhoads' dramatic presentation of John's Apocalypse. The Bible scholars, teachers, pastors, and authors from diverse communities of faith represented a wide spectrum of religious/moral conviction, ranging from liberal to conservative to in-between to some perhaps not really believing anything at all. When the lights went down, Rhoads stood alone on the spotlighted platform wearing a white robe with golden sash. The stage props consisted of a large paper scroll, a wooden staff, a golden trumpet, a golden bowl, and a table covered in white. For the next 90 minutes Rhoads was John the revelator telling all that he saw when, through an angel, Jesus revealed to him the things that must shortly come to pass (Rev. 1:1). Word for word from memory, Rhoads led us through the Apocalypse in dramatic flair. He spoke with passion, wonder, joy, exhortation, shouting, and whispers. You were literally spellbound at times.

Now, I've read Revelation many times in my life. In the months leading up to this occasion I had even read it through again, word by word in the original Greek. But I had never heard Revelation—never heard it orally, that is, apart from the few Sabbath morning or evangelistic series Scripture readings here and there from Revelation. I had never heard the whole book in one shot. Nor had I experienced it as oral drama. It was a moving moment. I was sitting on the floor along the side with my back against the wall, eyes closed, listening intently as we moved through one familiar passage to another. As my mind kept racing with anticipation to the next glorious scene, I found myself saying "Amen! Amen!" again and again. So much so that the man lying on the floor next to me would open his eyes every now and then and look at me as if to say, "What's with you?" It was then that I realized that not everyone might be experiencing this moment the same way as I was. I was watching it all unfold in my mind in the context of our unique Adventist understanding of Revelation and the perspective of the great controversy between Christ and Satan. My heart stirred with hope, and joy, and awe, but I wondered to myself how others were taking it in. Were they frightened? Did they see Jesus? How would God take this moment and bring it to spiritual life in their lives before the end?

In a few places Rhoads absolutely surprised me. His interpretation of a particular passage or phrase caught me off guard and provided a new insight. Particularly moving was his transition between chapter 20 and 21. He had just passionately interpreted the events following the millennium in which the devil and those outside the Holy City were thrown into the lake of fire—evil's abrupt and eternal end. Now there was a sustained pause. Everyone seemed to hold their breath as Rhoads seemed transfixed with a most glorious scene. A look of amazement and wonder spread across his face. His voice expressed that wonder as in quiet paced tones he spoke, "And I saw a new heaven and a new earth; for the first heaven and the first earth passed away, and there is no longer any sea. And I saw the holy city, new Jerusalem, coming down out of heaven from God, made ready as a bride adorned for her husband" (Rev. 21:1, 2). You could almost see the tears in his eyes. I could feel mine as well as the lump in my throat. What a glorious, glorious moment that will be!

Following this dramatic performance of the Apocalypse, a panel of four scholars debriefed the moment, describing its impact on them personally, and fielding questions from the audience. One of the panelists was Elizabeth Struthers Malbon. Malbon stated that she taught the Apocalypse and told how she, too, used dramatic reading as a way of helping students unlock its message. She spoke of how dramatically different Rhoads' interpretation of the Apocalypse was from hers. An example she picked was his transition between chapters 20 and 21. She shared how she interpreted it in contrast to Rhoads'. Rhoads had obviously caught her by surprise and stirred her up. Then Malbon said something very profound, something that each panelist and most everyone in the audience nodded their assent to: "I heard it orally, but it was a visual experience. I saw things in a new way!"

"I heard it orally, but it was a visual experience!" As I sat listening to Malbon, I couldn't help wondering about all the men and women who filled that crowded ballroom. To my surprise, the presentation startled most of them. Some spoke of its obvious gender bias against women or its overtly sexual overtones. Many felt it judgmental, and expressed anxiety. Others found it just one more academic exercise. Yet everyone there had perceived the Apocalypse in a new way. Not just heard it, but saw it in a new way.

In the course of time there will be another new reading of the Apocalypse and last-day events. Along with that new reading will be a new vision of self, God, reality, and all the moral spiritual issues packed in that ancient document. You and I will have a part in that dramatic new reading as the Holy Spirit of God will come with power and give life and vitality and vigor to what we herald from this book about Jesus, about last days, about the trinity of evil hellbent on destroying our planet. In the process of it all, we will unmask evil. Men and women from every walk of life and every corner of our world will be dumbstruck by what they now see. For many, their heart will stir with a passion to accept the new vision of truth and reality for themselves. They will hear the summons "Come out of her, My people" and obey it. What a glorious moment for God that will be.

So is the message of Esther. And so is the call to every one of us to allow the light of God's truth to unmask the Hamans in our lives so that we can then be humble servants in the hand of an incredibly awesome gracious God to unmask the Hamans of our world and the Hamans in the individual hearts we confront. Let there be a new reading. May God empower us to be His dramatic readers!

Once more we find ourselves *behind the seen*. In the opening clips of this grand unmasking, the main characters were all hiding something or something was being hidden from them. Haman and the king are not aware of Esther's identity or her relationship with Mordecai. The king does not know that Haman had it in for Mordecai. Nor does he realize how he has humiliated Haman by making him lead the Jew through the city in glorious display of honor. Esther, presumably, does not know of the events concerning Mordecai described in the previous chapter, since she makes no use of what would have been such welcome information.

"All the ingredients for a classical comedy are present."[27] Esther knows some things and not others. The same applies to Haman and the king. By the end of this gripping chapter all the unknowing bursts wide open. Suddenly every character in the unfolding drama has been brought up to speed.

God, however, knows everything from the beginning. Everybody else is in the dark. Only God sees and knows what's really taking place.

And only He knows the right timing for the unfolding of these critical events. From *behind the seen* He masterfully orchestrates events and uses His humble followers to bless the people of this world.

[1] Ralph Peters, "How Saddam Won This Round," *Newsweek,* Nov. 30, 1998.

[2] Ray C. Stedman, *The Queen and I* (Waco, Tex.: Word Books, 1977), p. 64.

[3] *Ibid.,* p. 72.

[4] *Ibid.*

[5] G. T. Dickinson, *Hidden Patterns and the Grand Design,* p. 106.

[6] Kenneth M. Craig, *Reading Esther* (Louisville: Westminster John Knox Press, 1995), p. 116.

[7] *Ibid.,* p. 117.

[8] *Ibid.,* pp. 117, 118.

[9] J. G. Baldwin, *Esther,* p. 93.

[10] Dickinson, p. 107.

[11] A. B. Luter and B. C. Davis, *God Behind the Seen,* p. 293.

[12] J. W. Hayford, *Redemption and Restoration,* p. 139.

[13] M. V. Fox, *Character and Ideology in the Book of Esther,* p. 183.

[14] A. M. Rodríguez, *Esther: A Theological Approach,* p. 112.

[15] Luter and Davis, p. 295.

[16] Craig, p. 115.

[17] Stedman, p. 73.

[18] *Ibid.,* p. 72.

[19] E. G. White, *Prophets and Kings,* pp. 605, 606.

[20] Rodríguez, p. 112.

[21] E. G. White, *The Great Controversy,* p. 604.

[22] *Ibid.,* p. 605.

[23] *Ibid.,* pp. 606, 607. (Italics supplied.)

[24] *Ibid.,* p. 612.

[25] Rodríguez, p. 53.

[26] Stedman, p. 74.

[27] J.W.H. Bos, *Ruth, Esther, Jonah,* p. 66.

CHAPTER NINE

HANG 10—ENOUGH IS NOT ENOUGH

Esther 9:1-17

Surfers are a wild breed. They live for the perfect wave. In between those perfect waves, they content themselves with shooting the curl, crashing down roaring mountains of water at 35 miles per hour, and just doing crazy things. For many, surfing and the meaning of life somehow coalesce. "We surf. Therefore, we are," they say. Or "May the Surf be with you." "And on the eighth day . . . God went surfing." A friend of mine has a middle-aged nephew who literally exists for those perfect waves. He lives alone in a shabby little hut on a beautiful Hawaiian beach. Nothing else matters. Just the surf—just the thrill of the ride.

Expert surfers work on special techniques such as one-footing, standing on their heads (can you imagine?), or hanging 10. Hanging 10 in surfer lingo means surfing while curling all 10 toes over one edge of the board. It's a feat of balance and guts. Most of us can't imagine standing in the middle of a surfboard without it tipping over, let alone having our feet hang over one edge while leaning way back over the other in counterbalance—all the while cutting through a curl at breakneck speed.

Although Esther probably never rode a surfboard, she knew all about hanging 10. To her, though, hanging 10 did not mean curling her toes over the edge of a surfboard. She took it literally as "hanging 10" men.[1] She wanted to hang the bodies of all 10 of Haman's sons on the very gallows on which their father had died. "If it pleases the king," she pleads, "let tomorrow also be granted to the Jews who are in Susa to do according to the edict of today; and let Haman's ten sons be hanged on the gallows" (Esther 9:13).

By now Haman had been executed, and Mordecai, together with Esther, had generated a counterdecree allowing the Jews to defend themselves against their enemies (Esther 8:8-14). The two decrees converged on the thirteenth of Adar. On that day two diametrically opposed groups of people, on the basis of one or the other of those irrevocable edicts, sought to annihilate each other. Now that fateful day had arrived. But "when the enemies of the Jews hoped to gain the mastery over them, it was turned to the contrary so that the Jews themselves gained the mastery over those who hated them" (Esther 9:1). The upside-down cake had finally turned right side up.

When King Ahasuerus heard the details of the daylong battle of Adar 13 between the Jews and their opponents, he seemed surprised that the Jews had killed 510 people in Susa alone. "If that's the case," he wondered out loud, "how many did they kill throughout the rest of the provinces of Persia?" (see verse 12). When the reports all came in, that body count would reach an astonishing 75,000 (verse 16)! At this point, you might expect the king to say, "Whew! That's enough! No more killing! You're safe now, Esther. We've taken care of the problem." But he doesn't. As if reading Esther's mind, Ahasuerus asks, "Now what? Is there anything else you want done? Just tell me, and I'll do it for you" (see verse 12).

An incredible question received an equally amazing answer! Esther surprises us with her gutsy request—"let tomorrow also be granted to the Jews who are in Susa to do according to the edict today; and let Haman's ten sons be hanged on the gallows" (verse 13). Even though her situation far surpasses anything she could have imagined a few months earlier, she's not satisfied. Esther wants more dead bodies! She asks the king for permission to allow the killing in Susa to continue another day and to have Haman's 10 sons—who had already been killed—impaled on the very same pencil-sharp gallows their father had built seven months earlier.

We need to catch the visual imagery here. A second day of grisly fighting and mounting death toll. Ten already-dead bodies harpooned on high gibbets so that they hang out to bloat and rot in the sun, grow maggots, and be picked apart by birds. Disgusting, isn't it?

About now most of us wish that the story of Esther had ended with the hanging of Haman. It was easy to feel good about Esther then. The heroes had acted with noble bearing, and the archvillain, Haman, had received just punishment.[2] End of story.

127

Surprisingly, Esther shows no mercy toward either Haman or his family. First, she and Mordecai wrote a second edict that allowed the Jews to kill their enemies together with their wives and children and to plunder their property (Esther 8:11). Second, she impaled the 10 sons of Haman on the gallows and asked for a second day to continue the massacre (Esther 9:13). Finally, the Jews joyfully celebrated after the bloodbath ended (verse 17).[3] Such carnage and gloating don't make Esther look good.[4] Her request for a second day of slaughter and hanging 10 (Esther 9:11-15) raises our civilized and politically correct eyebrows. It appears bloodthirsty, inhumane, pagan. Something out of the Dark Ages. Many read these things in Esther and come away confused or appalled over the moral attitude it appears to have—interracial/religious hostility, vengefulness, and disrespect for the life of innocent people.[5] It is the stuff that modern critical scholarship points toward as examples of the cultural conditioning of Scripture and how its words are mere human ones—the words of an ancient people who understood God in light of the values and moralities of an ancient world.

For sure, Esther's story is a natural springboard for a discussion of vengeance and retaliation.[6] When the tables turn, human hearts often seek to get even for the wrongs experienced. It happens all the time. "One of the most dreadful repercussions of oppression is that it may recreate the former victims into a mirror image of the former oppressors."[7] Is Esther an example of what to do—or not to do?

Some suggest that "Esther's personality has evolved into the near-opposite of what it was at the start. Once sweet and compliant, she is now steely and unbending, even harsh."[8] Is that what happened with her? Did "a malignant spirit of revenge" now motivate her? Did she turn harder, blunter, even crueler? What about all the killing? Doesn't it fly in the face of the Sermon on the Mount? Doesn't it imply fierce nationalism and unblushing vindictiveness? Is her story just another product of human history?

When Enough Is Not Enough

The closing moments of the 100-hour land battle of the 1991 Persian Gulf War found American armor divisions, under the command of General Norman Schwarzkopf, waiting just 150 miles south of Baghdad. By that time in the conflict the Iraqi Army was in full retreat and Saddam Hussein's celebrated Republican Guard was racing to cross the Euphrates before it was too late. Their haste turned to horror, though, when they ran smack-dab into the waiting, state-of-the-art American tanks. The ensuing tank battle thoroughly devastated any remaining Iraqi resistance.

Now what? On to Baghdad? Hang Saddam Hussein?

That's what the American generals wanted. Within hours it would be over for good. And so their tanks idled as they waited for the go-ahead. All they needed to finish the job was a nod from United States president George Bush. But Bush and other politicians deemed a march on Baghdad politically incorrect and risky in a region where U.S. motives are suspect. Instead they struck a deal, deciding to contain the Iraqi dictator. It was the best of both worlds, they thought. Saddam Hussein would be bottled up for good and the Americans would avoid any unnecessary humiliation of Arabs.

More than a decade later the United States and sympathetic Arab countries in the region were still living with Saddam Hussein. He's thrown one temper tantrum after another and, for all intents and purposes, is still quite a threat to the region's peace and security. How many times have we said to ourselves, "We should have finished the job! We should have gone in there and cleaned house while we had the chance"?

It appears that Esther also understood what the generals south of Baghdad did. She grasped the principle of doing everything possible—of never quitting—until one has secured the final victory against a mortal enemy. Otherwise, evil will come back not only to haunt you but to destroy you once and for all. That was a principle Israel's King Saul hadn't grasped. He hadn't done a thorough job with the Amalekites. Instead he brought Agag back for the victory party. Now in Esther's day another generation of God's people were still struggling with the same enemy. The enmity was in the genes. Once again it turned deadly. What Esther understood was that while Haman was dead, the evil he intended was very much alive.[9] The moral spiritual reality was that it was "not a people but a way of life that was to be destroyed—a way of life that constituted a powerful and relentless threat to God's rule."[10] That same powerful, relentless threat against God had once again focused on His people. It was a matter of life or death.

Before we go on, I want to note four things about the way Esther and her people responded to the sinister genocidal plot Haman unleashed. First, the decree Esther and Mordecai drew up together allowed only for self-defense. The Jews received the right to fight against those who "sought their harm" (Esther 9:2). The phrase "sought their harm" refers to those who would actually fight the Jews, not merely those who were hostile. No evidence in the text suggests that the Jews took the initiative and attacked the Gentiles.[11] Their only goal was to repulse those who might assault them. According to the record, however, more than 70,000 were foolish enough to do exactly that. Or shall we say, more than 70,000 were filled with impassioned hatred to the point where they vented their feelings in a burst of ethnic cleansing.

Second, the Jews showed remarkable restraint during the ensuing battles. Three times the narrative tells us that, after defeating their enemies, the Jews did not take the plunder (verses 10, 15, 16). They had the freedom to seize the property of those they defeated. The edict not only allowed it, but it was the accepted custom of the times. But they didn't take one lamb, one gold piece, one innocent life. Although they defended themselves, they went no further. They deliberately restrained from plundering the property belonging to the dead, suggesting that the Jews did not kill the women and children. Rather, they left the property for their use.[12]

Joyce Baldwin offers a helpful insight here: "Though in the book of Esther the tables had turned on those who would have killed the Jews, the Jews had behind them all the theological conditioning provided by their scriptures, and their understanding of permission to avenge themselves would have been adjusted accordingly."[13] Furthermore, she writes, "the deliberate decision not to enrich themselves at the expense of their enemies would not go unnoticed in a culture where victors were expected to take the spoil. The very novelty of such self-denial would be remarked upon and remembered, and taken as proof of the upright motives of the Jewish communities."[14]

Third, there still remained dangerous enemies. The results of the second day's fighting in Susa indicate that significant pockets of zealous anti-Jewish resistance still lurked in the capital city even after the fighting of the first day. God's people wouldn't be truly safe until the eradication of those hardened, headstrong foes.

Finally, the visual imagery of "hanging 10" on a grisly gibbet, as well as the issue of genealogy (they were Haman's sons), serves to reinforce the fact that God's enemies are to be pursued and destroyed to the very last one. There must be complete victory or there is no victory at all. At the heart of that visual image is a clear public message—"What these men and their father stood for will never be allowed again!"[16] It's like the slogan we so often hear about the Holocaust—"Never again!"

But while Esther's actions obviously point in this direction, they also hint at a larger eschatological picture. "Hanging 10" foretells the moment when evil will not just be exposed for what it really is, but entirely defeated as well. As Rodríguez writes: "A Christian reading of Esther must take into consideration the book's perception of evil. Esther is a story of hope and courage. It presupposes that evil is by its own nature defeatable. It is that conviction that keeps the protagonists working together in very ingenious ways to put an end to a most threatening evil plan. The overthrow of a universal threat points beyond itself to the ultimate defeat of evil."[17] "The defeat of evil in Esther is a pointer to a future in which evil will be finally eradicated from the world. Esther makes it clear that evil is defeatable. Its defeat reaches almost eschatological dimensions in the book."[18]

It reminds us of Nahum's startling yet hope-filled prophecy. Speaking of God's whirlwind judgment against wicked Nineveh, Nahum writes: "With an overwhelming flood he will make an end of Nineveh; he will pursue his foes into darkness. Whatever they plot against the Lord he will bring to an end; trouble will not come a second time" (Nahum 1:8, 9, NIV). *The Living Bible* puts verse 9 this way: "He will stop you with one blow; he won't need to strike again." "Affliction will not rise up a second time" the New King James Version reads. Many commentators assert the eschatological promise symbolized in God's complete destruction of Nineveh. Evil and sin as we so painfully know it in our world will someday be decisively dealt with. The end of evil and sin will be complete and unequivocal. God will not need to strike again. Nor will God's people be afflicted or threatened anymore.

It's All in the Roll

Our family recently purchased a new Risk game. Risk is that world domination board game in which your armies battle one another till only one player is left. This battle for global domination spills over several world theaters—North America, South America, Africa, Europe, Russia, Asia, and the South Pacific. Each player begins with equal amounts of infantry, cavalry, and artillery. Fate, though, hangs in the roll of the dice. Risk has five dice, three red and two white. The attacker always gets the three red dice. The defender just the two white dice. For all intents and purposes, the attacker, in principle at least, always has the advantage. After all, there's always one more die to tip the scale. During battle both sides roll. The higher numbers rolled win over lower numbers. Equal numbers mean equal losses on both sides. The attacker's third die provides the added statistical advantage of a higher number.

My youngest son is quite gutsy in Risk, always attacking, always taking risks. Loving to roll the dice and make his opponents squirm, he will extend himself far across the board, gaining more and more territory. His aggressive tactic usually pays off, though. By the time others get around to their turn, they don't have much left to fight with. If the tide happens to turn against him, though, the reality of three dice rolling against his two dice creates real anxiety. At such moments he'll keep shaking and shaking his two white dice, afraid to roll. Afraid the numbers will come up wrong. Those attacking get impatient. "Come on! Just roll the dice! Don't take so long." As we wait for him I have often said, "Hey, it's all in the roll of the dice! There's nothing you can do about it, except roll. So just roll!" It never does any good, though. "It's all in the roll of the dice" sounds too fatalistic for a 9-year-old.

The book of Esther tells us that Haman threw dice in his high-stakes bid for domination over the Jews. "For Haman the son of Hammedatha, the Agagite, the adversary of the Jews, had schemed against the Jews to destroy them, and had cast Pur, that is the lot, to disturb them and destroy them" (Esther 9:24). It was real-life Risk! We get the fuller picture in chapter 3: "In the first month, which is the month of Nisan, in the twelfth year of King Ahasuerus, Pur, that is the lot, was cast before Haman from day to day and from month to month, until the twelfth month, that is the month Adar" (verse 7). In other words, Haman cast lots again and again to establish which month of the year would be best for his genocide plan. He then cast lots in order to establish which day in that "lucky month" would be the "lucky day."

Just imagine it—Haman rolled the die to determine the exact day of extermination. Through "pur" he led himself to believe that he had fixed the fate of the Jews once and for all. The gods were on his side. Fate was in his favor. His evil scheme would triumph. It was all in the roll of the die!

But Esther's underlying message is that God had something different in mind for His threatened people. The unseen God doesn't care how the dice roll. He has determined a different fate for His people and for our world. Evil is not only defeatable—it *will* be defeated. What are the chances that evil will succeed? None! The devil rages across our earth in great wrath, because he knows he has a short time. It is we who need to be convinced of the final outcome.

We can best explain the plural form of the name of the feast Purim as designating the two "fates" decreed for the Jews: one by Haman and his gods, the other by the God of heaven. The feast celebrates God's mysterious work from within history that brings salvation and joy and rest to His people.[19] No matter how evil now seems to have the upper hand, its triumph is not in the roll of the dice. The outcome rests in the hands of a loving and powerful God whose sovereign providence will create a different reality.

Like Esther, the book of Revelation depicts evil forces threatening the very existence of God's people. In fact, all of Scripture—Revelation and Daniel in particular—and *The Great Controversy* declare the complete defeat of evil and its final eradication from the world. Together

133

they envision a total collapse of evil and the ending of the struggle between Christ and Satan (Rev. 18-20). " 'For behold, the day is coming, burning like a furnace; and all the arrogant and every evildoer will be chaff; and the day that is coming will set them ablaze,' says the Lord of hosts, 'so that it will leave them neither root nor branch' " (Mal. 4:1).

"Be still before the Lord and wait patiently for him; do not fret when men succeed in their ways, when they carry out their wicked schemes. Refrain from anger and turn from wrath; do not fret—it leads only to evil. For evil men will be cut off, but those who hope in the Lord will inherit the land. A little while, and the wicked will be no more; though you look for them, they will not be found. . . . The wicked plot against the righteous and gnash their teeth at them; but the Lord laughs at the wicked; for he knows their day is coming. . . . Wait for the Lord, and keep his way. He will exalt you to inherit the land; when the wicked are cut off, you will see it" (Ps. 37:7-34, NIV).

It's Not My Problem—Or Is It?

During the summer of 1998 *Newsweek* ran a series of articles on Steven Spielberg's gritty blood-and-guts blockbuster epic *Saving Private Ryan.*[20] It's a story about the very down-to-earth personal travails of war. Military leaders send a weary World War II squadron behind enemy lines to save a Private James Ryan, the youngest of four enlisted brothers and the only apparent survivor. He's missing in action. Having parachuted behind enemy lines, he's in imminent danger. Where is he? How is he? According to *Newsweek,* the focus of *Saving Private Ryan* is on the little guy. A mere private, he is a seeming nobody in the great sweep of the Normandy invasion and of a global conflict stretching across multiple theaters. The movie brings the whole focus on war from the global to the individual. Spielberg concentrates on individual soldiers in the great war machine rather than the war itself. In other words, he puts a face on the battle—the face of a nobody. It is not a general or a major or a captain, just a little guy like you and me. It's as if to say, "It's easy to look at the global picture, the cosmic picture, and forget the personal battle." War is very real for the little guy out there in the trenches.

134

How true that is with our battle against evil and sin. Reading Esther makes it easy for us to get swept away with that larger picture and somehow come away feeling we're lost in the crowd. God wants us to read Esther very personally, though. Esther's struggle against Haman and the evil he embodied was intensely personal. She had to look him in the eye, face him off, and say what needed to be said. It needs to be that way with us as well. "Hanging 10" suggests something important about spiritual warfare and intercession on a personal level.

First, we need to grasp the reality of personal struggle with the powers of darkness outside us and the evil within us. "Finally, be strong in the Lord, and in the strength of His might. Put on the full armor of God, that you may be able to stand firm against the schemes of the devil. For our struggle is not against flesh and blood, but against the rulers, against the powers, against the world forces of this darkness, against spiritual forces of wickedness in the heavenly places" (Eph. 6:10-12).

Paul highlights the highly personal dimensions of this reality in Romans 7:14-24, in which he tells of "not practicing what I would like to do, but I am doing the very thing I hate. . . . For I know that nothing good dwells in me, that is, in my flesh; for the wishing is present in me, but the doing of the good is not. For the good that I wish, I do not do; but I practice the very evil that I do not wish. But if I am doing the very thing I do not wish, I am no longer the one doing it, but sin which dwells in me. . . . Wretched man that I am! Who will set me free from the body of this death?" He goes on to write how it is the Holy Spirit alone who brings victory (Rom. 8:1-11). That is why he states that "those who belong to Christ Jesus have crucified the flesh with its passions and desires" (Gal. 5:24).

Second, we must understand the principle of doing everything possible—of never quitting—until the final victory is secured. In gaining the mastery over evil, shall we hold back or finish the job? Ellen White tells us that "it is a perilous thing to allow an unchristian trait to live in the heart. One cherished sin will, little by little, debase the character, bringing all its nobler powers into subjection to the evil desire. The removal of one safeguard from the conscience, the indulgence of one evil habit, one neglect of the high claims of duty, breaks down the defenses of the soul and opens the way for Satan to come in and lead us astray."[21]

In her book *Pilgrim at Tinker Creek* Annie Dillard writes: "A couple summers ago I was walking along the edge of the island to see what I could see in the water, and mainly to scare frogs. Frogs have an inelegant way of taking off from invisible positions on the bank just ahead of your feet, in dire panic, emitting a froggy 'Yike!' and splashing into the water. Incredibly, this amused me, and, incredibly, it amuses me still. As I walked along the grassy edge of the island, I got better and better at seeing frogs both in and out of water. I learned to recognize, slowing down, the difference in texture of the light reflected from mudbank, water, grass, or frog. Frogs were flying all around me. At the end of the island I noticed a small green frog. He was exactly half in and half out of the water, looking like a schematic diagram of an amphibian, and he didn't jump.

"He didn't jump; I crept closer. At last I knelt on the island's winterkilled grass, lost, dumbstruck, staring at the frog in the creek just four feet away. He as a very small frog with wide, dull eyes. And just as I looked at him, he slowly crumpled and began to sag. The spirit vanished from his eyes as if snuffed. His skin emptied and drooped; his very skull seemed to collapse and settle like a kicked tent. He was shrinking before my very eyes like a deflating football. I watched the taut, glistening skin on his shoulders ruck, and rumple, and fall. Soon, part of his skin, formless as a pricked balloon, lay in floating folds like bright scum on top of the water: it was a monstrous and terrible thing. I gaped bewildered, appalled. An oval shadow hung in the water behind the drained frog: then the shadow glided away. The frog skin started to sink.

"I had read about the water bug, but never seen one. 'Giant water bug' is really the name of the creature, which is an enormous, heavy-bodied brown beetle. It eats insects, tadpoles, fish, and frogs. Its grasping forelegs are mighty and hooked inward. It seizes a victim with these legs, hugs it tight, and paralyzes it with enzymes injected during a vicious bite. That one bite is the only bite it ever takes. Through the puncture shoot the poisons that dissolves the victim's muscles and bones and organs—all but the skin—and through it the giant water bug sucks out the victim's body, reduced to a juice. . . . I had been kneeling on the island grass; when the unrecognizable flap of frog skin settled on the creek bottom, swaying, I stood up and brushed the knees of my pants. I couldn't catch my breath."[22]

Like the bug, our sins can paralyze our spirit. And even though the effects may not show immediately, sooner or later they suck the life out of us. Through the power of the living Lord Jesus, we must "hang 10." As Oswald Chambers writes, there must be a "cocrucifixion." "Have I made this decision about sin—that it must be killed right out in me? It takes a long time to come to a moral decision about sin, but it is the great moment in my life when I do decide that just as Jesus Christ died for the sin of the world, so sin must die out in me, not be curbed or suppressed or counteracted, but crucified. No one can bring anyone else to this decision. . . . Haul yourself up, take a time alone with God, make the moral decision and say—'Lord, identify me with Thy death until I know that sin is dead in me.'"[23]

But then there's our personal struggle with the evil that we find in the lives of others and how they treat or threaten us. Swindoll calls this the "retaliation syndrome."[24] It's the moral erosion that takes place on the part of both the offender and the offended. Someone offends us or mistreats us to the place that in the course of time thoughts of retaliation intensify in our own hearts. "Then, one day, the tables are turned. The enormous cat becomes the mouse. The prisoner gets the gun. The victim gains the upper hand. This provides the opportunity to get even. And if there is nothing to stop him, watch out! The offended retaliates against the offender with full-scale vengeance."[25]

This growth of intensity on both sides is exactly what happened between the Jews and Gentiles of ancient Persia. The Jews experienced an escalating hatred. Anti-Semitism ran rampant. Through it all God's people experienced an increased sense of helplessness and defenselessness. Then one day the tables turned. Thankfully, though, they applied spiritual and moral restraint before the fires of revenge got out of control. As we have already learned, the Jews had behind them all the theological conditioning provided by Scripture, and they adjusted their understanding of permission to avenge themselves accordingly. The retaliation syndrome did not occur. They did not plunder their enemies' possessions or destroy their families.

What is it that stops the retaliation syndrome? Only one thing: self-control under the Spirit of God and trust in the final work of God to bring a full end to evil and avenge the wrongs done to His children. We get that view from Scripture, especially stories such as that of Esther. "Do not repay anyone evil for evil. Be careful to do what is right in the eyes of everybody. If it is possible, as far as it depends on you, live at peace with everyone. Do not take revenge, my friends, but leave room for God's wrath, for it is written, 'It is mine to avenge; I will repay,' says the Lord. On the contrary: 'If your enemy is hungry, feed him; if he is thirsty, give him something to drink. In doing this, you will heap burning coals on his head.' Do not be overcome by evil, but overcome evil with good" (Rom. 12:17-21, NIV).

Not only did the Jews gain mastery over their enemies—they achieved it over themselves.[26] The Jews were not out of control, but in control. They defended themselves but went no further. Responding to evil has a personal, social, and a cosmic dimension. Between our own hearts and the great issues in the great controversy between Christ and Satan are people.

Who Will Deliver?

In February 1998 a tornado splintered a Kissimmee, Florida, wood-frame house and grabbed 18-month-old Jonathan Waldick. But the deadly twister seemed to have a change of heart when confronted with a child. The same winds that had snatched Jonathan snapped the top off a nearby oak and deposited him in its protective branches. There the baby lay nestled safely in his mattress while around him the world seemed to be coming to an end. Hail and rain pelted the ground. The concrete house next door crumbled. Giant trees snapped. And Jonathan received only a bump on his head.

Shirley Driver, the child's great-grandmother, didn't know that. Taking care of him at the time, she had been sleeping in her bed with Jonathan's 4-year-old sister, Destiny, when the storm hit. Driver woke up to find Destiny safe, but where was Jonathan? It appeared that the terrible answer was under the huge pile of debris.

Word of the tragedy spread. At Lakeview Elementary School (an emergency shelter) in St. Cloud, Florida, tornado survivors talked about a baby whisked out of its mother's arms and into the sky. Ron Vernelson, who was helping his son next door, came over to Driver's house to help search for Jonathan. Other rescuers also arrived. "We started looking, but there was no bedroom," Vernelson later said. After combing through rubble for 40 minutes, one of the men spotted something at eye level in the oak branches. "I think I see a foot," he said. They investigated, and soon they saw the rest of Jonathan. His eyes were wide open, but he wasn't making a sound. "He's dead," the deputy said. Then the foot moved. "I kept calling his name, and he started to whimper," Vernelson reported. "I said, 'the baby is alive.'" Another volunteer—a slimmer man—slid through the tangled mass of boards and limbs to pull Jonathan out. "The mattress saved him. He was just lying on the mattress sideways."[27] But the mattress didn't save that little baby boy—God did! And it is God alone who graciously and sovereignly saves us from the overmastering power of evil. As Rodríguez asserts, the Jewish festival of Purim "does not celebrate the victory of the Jews over their enemies. The feast does not celebrate human power."[28] It praises the mighty power of God.

Ellen White tells us that *"God wrought marvelously for His penitent people; and a counter decree issued by the king, allowing them to fight for their lives, was rapidly communicated to every part of the realm. . . . On the day appointed for their destruction, 'the Jews gathered themselves together in their cities throughout all the provinces of the king Ahasuerus, to lay hand on such as sought their hurt: and no man could withstand them; for the fear of them fell upon all the people.' Angels that excel in strength had been commissioned by God to protect His people while they 'stood for their lives'* (Esther 9:2, 16)."[29]

Behind the seen the threatening power of evil lurks on a very personal level in individual human hearts.

Behind the seen in the big-risk controversy between Christ and Satan there is One who is able to deliver those who put their trust in Him.

Behind the seen there is One who determines destiny no matter how human beings roll the dice or no matter the odds. Satan has rolled. Jesus has rolled. The decision is yours.

"And they overcame him because of the blood of the Lamb and because of the word of their testimony" (Rev. 12:11).

---

[1] A. B. Luter and B. C. Davis, *God Behind the Seen*, p. 321.
[2] G. T. Dickinson, *Hidden Patterns and the Grand Design*, p. 120.
[3] A. M. Rodríguez, *Esther: A Theological Approach*, p. 12.
[4] Dickinson, p. 121.
[5] Rodríguez, p. 12.
[6] C. R. Swindoll, *Esther: A Woman of Strength and Dignity*, p. 156.
[7] J.W.H. Bos, *Ruth, Esther, Jonah*, p. 69.
[8] M. V. Fox, *Character and Ideology in the Book of Esther*, p. 203.
[9] Bos, p. 68.
[10] E. Peterson, *Five Smooth Stones for Pastoral Work*, p. 171.
[11] Rodríguez, p. 14.
[12] Swindoll, p. 163.
[13] J. G. Baldwin, *Esther*, p. 102.
[14] *Ibid.*, p. 105.
[15] J. W. Hayford, *Redemption and Restoration*, p. 150.
[16] Swindoll, p. 163.
[17] Rodríguez, p. 112.
[18] *Ibid.*, p. 107.
[19] *Ibid.*, p. 29.
[20] Jon Meacham, "Caught in the Line of Fire," *Newsweek*, July 13, 1998, pp. 48-55; David Ansen, "Celluloid Soldiers," *Newsweek*, July 13, 1998, pp. 52, 53; Stephen E. Ambrose, "The Kids Who Changed the World," *Newsweek*, July 13, 1998, p. 59.
[21] Ellen G. White, *Patriarchs and Prophets* (Mountain View, Calif.: Pacific Press Pub. Assn., 1890), p. 452.
[22] Annie Dillard, *Pilgrim at Tinker Creek* (New York: Harper's Magazine Press, 1974), pp. 5, 6.
[23] Oswald Chambers, *My Utmost for His Highest*, April 10.
[24] Swindoll, p. 164.
[25] *Ibid.*, p. 165.
[26] *Ibid.*, p. 163.
[27] Susan Jacobson, "Sucked Out of Bed and Into a Tree, Baby Survives Storm," *Orlando Sentinel*, Feb. 24, 1998.
[28] Rodríguez, p. 28.
[29] E. G. White, *Prophets and Kings*, p. 602. (Italics supplied.)

CHAPTER TEN

A PUR-FECT DAY FOR A FOREVER PARTY

Esther 9:20-32

Through the centuries the Feast of Purim has been one of the most festive of all the Jewish holidays.[1] Because the events recorded in Esther "turned for them from sorrow into gladness and from mourning into a holiday" (Esther 9:22), both Mordecai and Esther commanded the Jews (verses 20, 21, 29-32) to make the fourteenth and fifteenth of Adar "days of feasting and joy, days for sending presents of food to one another and gifts to the poor" (verse 22, NEB). So Purim became an annual holiday filled with merrymaking, feasting, drinking, and reading the megillah (the scroll of Esther). In time it has turned into a wildly hilarious celebration that includes boisterous and ironic songs and a lot of often bizarre symbolism. Centuries ago Jews in Frankfurt would craft a wax house on the center platform of the synagogue (called the *bimoh*) complete with wax figures of Haman, his wife, Zeresh, and the hangman. They set it on fire as soon as the reader began reading from the book of Esther.[2] Another old custom involved making an effigy of Haman that the celebrants would hang and burn at the reading of Esther.[3] As far back as the fifth century some charged the Jews with burning the cross and a figure of Jesus on Purim. Such slander led to attacks upon the Jews by their Christian neighbors. In time, under pressure, such customs disappeared, including the practice of lighting 10 memorial candles on Purim for Haman's 10 sons.

To this day, when they read the book of Esther on Purim, Jewish children come dressed in costumes. Purim is a great time of masquerade, a moment of satire and parody. Even adults dress up. Surprisingly, some of the costumes worn involve some kind of role reversal. For instance, Jewish men may wear women's clothes and Jewish women may wear men's clothes (something normally and stringently forbidden in Scripture and Jewish ethic). Gentile clothing, too, is often worn during Purim.[4] In addition, one may observe food snatching, hitting, and drunkenness.[5]

Because the book of Esther records so many drinking parties, Jewish culture actually encourages the drinking of alcoholic beverages during Purim. Tradition tells people to drink to the point that they are unable to distinguish between the statements "blessed be Mordecai" and "cursed be Haman."[6] Drunken people get disoriented, their world becomes topsy-turvy, and they fall. The ironic twists and turns in Esther and the ultimate fall of Haman point to just such disorder and reversal.

When they reach the moment for reading Esther, many have some sort of noisemaker: pots and pans, anything that will groan or rattle or screech or bang.[7] The atmosphere reflects that of an old-time melodrama. Everyone cheers the heroes (Mordecai and Esther), and they boo and hiss and stomp their feet when the book mentions the name of Haman. Actually, when the reader reaches Haman's name in chapter 3, the people try to drown it out. In joyful obedience to the Scripture's command to "blot out the memory of Amalek" (Ex. 17:14) and in angry recognition of Haman's family resemblance to Amalek, they bang, rattle, and bash the noisemakers. Some write Haman's name on bits of paper, then gleefully tear them up and scatter them to the winds. Or they may ink his name on the soles of their shoes, which they joyfully rub upon the floor. Some also scribble the names of later Hamans—monsters of anti-Semitism or of other tyrannies—who seem to be spiritual descendants of Amalek.[8]

Clearly, for many Jews, the scroll of Esther presents a literary joke. The book's message becomes a mobilization of hilarity and humor to cure the soul of fear and to shatter the pompous pretensions of all tyranny. The story of Esther is, indeed, the intertwining of two jokes. In one of them, Haman's efforts to impale Mordecai, destroy the Jews, and elevate himself are rewarded with precise irony: Haman himself is impaled, his own party massacred, and Mordecai and all the Jews are elevated to great power and honor.

The other joke is similar in structure, though sketched in ink less bloody: King Ahasuerus gets the whole story going by deposing Queen Vashti so that he and all other husbands will never again have to take orders from their wives. He ends the tale by taking orders precisely from his wife—the new Queen Esther. As Haman's murderous anti-Semitism carries him to his own death, so Ahasuerus's contemptuous anti-feminism brings him to his own stultification. The joke is on the tyrant.[9] No wonder some Jewish scholars will say, "God forbid that God should appear in such a story!"[10] One speculates, too, if God ever appears in Purim as well.

Purim is also a time for sending food and gifts for the needy and the Purim feast (Esther 9:22). Each individual has an obligation to send two portions of food to at least one person. The food should be such that it can be eaten without further preparation.

Each person has to eat, drink, and be especially merry on Purim. On the night of the fourteenth one should rejoice and make some kind of feast.[11]

An Unfading Memory

We may chuckle at the buffoonery, parody, and laughter that have come to be a part of the Jewish tradition of Purim, but the original purpose for Purim was eloquent: "So these days were to be remembered and celebrated throughout every generation, every family, every province, and every city; and these days of Purim were not to fail from among the Jews, or their memory fade from their descendants" (verse 28). Purim was to be a memory enhancer. The festival was to help God's people keep in touch with the existential heart of their fragile, often double, existence (in the world but not of the world) in an alternately indifferent and hostile world.[12] Although threatened with destruction, they were not destroyed. Marvelously, God had been *behind the seen* and working in their behalf.

The experience of God's people during the time of Esther was not unlike that of Fyodor Dostoyevsky when he faced imminent execution and Nicholas I, Russia's czar, reprieved him at the last moment. After long months of imprisonment in St. Petersburg's infamous Peter and Paul Fortress for revolutionary activities, soldiers led Dostoyevsky to a public place of execution and lined him up with his fellow prisoners. A priest in full burial vestments and carrying a Bible and a cross met Dostoyevsky and his colleagues. An ominous drumroll filled the air as

143

the writer stumbled in the snow past lines of soldiers. The atmosphere was tense. Everything indicated momentary execution. Three stakes stood in the frozen ground, and behind them rested a line of carts full of empty coffins.

Up to this moment Dostoyevsky had no idea he was going to die. It was simply unbelievable. Everything was happening so fast. Did he really have only a few minutes left among the living? "It's not possible that they mean to execute us," Dostoyevsky whispered in a faltering voice to his compatriot Durov. But Durov only pointed in silence to the waiting carts.

"Present arms!" Again the drumroll sounded ominously across Semyonovsky Square. An officer came forward and began to read the sentences in a great hurry to the prisoners who stood in their summer clothes in the freezing weather. One by one he condemned them to death before a firing squad. Then they received white shirts with hoods and long sleeves. The priest faced the prisoners and quoted from the Bible. "The wages of sin are death," he intoned. The soldiers leveled their rifles at the condemned men. Tension mounted with every passing moment. But then, at the very second the soldiers were to fire, a courier raced into the square yelling, "Wait! Wait!" He carried a last-moment reprieve from the czar. The Russian leader had actually given it some time before, but withheld it until the last minute to jerk Dostoyevsky and his compatriots around and demonstrate Nicholas's great mercy. It was all sadistic mental torture. The prisoner standing next to Dostoyevsky couldn't handle it and went mad. Guards hauled Dostoyevsky off to four years of hard labor in Siberia.[13]

That terrible mock execution proved a crucial moment of insight for Dostoyevsky. It was an existential turning point, forever changing his life and helping him grasp the heart of the gospel. Dostoyevsky relates that the worst thing during those frightful moments was the constant, nagging thought, *Think if I don't die. Imagine that I am turned back to life, imagine how endless it will seem. A whole eternity! And this eternity will belong to me! Then I will live every minute as a century, without losing any of it, and I will keep an account of each minute and not waste a moment.*[14] For the first time in his life Dostoyevsky "felt intensely the divine mystery of existence, *the grace of life.*"[15]

The Feast of Purim was to remind God's people in following generations of just such a kind of psycho-emotional wrenching reversal. They must remember that "life . . . is celebrated as a joyous gift, snatched unbelievably from the gates of death and hell. A people who had faced the possibility of not being are emphatically alive."[16] Esther presents the overwhelming threat of holocaust, but it never happens. The result is bewildering shock followed by wildly celebrative joy. A spontaneous celebration. Celebration burst out when they first learned of the second decree (Esther 8:16). Then it exploded again when the tables turned and their enemies were fully defeated (Esther 9:17). Joy and feasting marked both moments—a holiday spirit. The four Hebrew words used in these passages *(simchah, sason, mishteh, towb)* together point to a very earthly moment of joy, exultation, gaiety, and pleasure (Esther 8:16; 9:17, 18, 19, 22, 27). They emphasize a full sensory experience that would link heart and body and emotion. Interestingly, the word for festival in Esther is *mishteh,* meaning drinking party. Each of the banquets recorded had a lot of drinking taking place.

God's people were going to die. They knew it was coming. The executioner had already called out his "Ready! Aim!" The ominous drumroll jerked their psyche. Tension ran high. So when the unseen sovereign God miraculously intervened in their behalf, no one had to tell them to celebrate. It was spontaneous and vibrant. They gave gifts because they now realized life itself was a gift (Esther 9:22). Now God commanded them through Esther and Mordecai to choose the very days when they would have been annihilated and exterminated and turn those days from sadness and mourning to rejoicing and celebration in acknowledgment of the change of events. And they must never, never forget!

It makes me think of the glorious picture of God's redeemed people in Psalm 126: "When the Lord brought back the captive ones of Zion, we were like those who dream. Then our mouth was filled with laughter, and our tongue with joyful shouting; then they said among the nations, 'The Lord has done great things for them.' The Lord has done great things for us; we are glad. Restore our captivity, O Lord, as the streams in the South. Those who sow in tears shall reap with joyful shouting. He who goes to and fro weeping, carrying his bag of seed, shall indeed come again with a shout of joy, bringing his sheaves with him."

You don't need to tell redeemed people to celebrate. They just do it! The mouth easily fills with laughter, the eye with tears, the tongue with joyful shouting. Nor do you have to remind them to praise their liberator. It happened in the Gulf War following the 100 hours of Desert Storm. On February 27, 1991, columns of liberating troops rolled up the battered wreckage-strewn expressway leading into Kuwait City. Civilian cars formed a convoy around them, horns honking, flags waving. Crowds along the way danced and chanted, *"Allah akbar! Allah akbar!"* "U.S.A.! U.S.A.!" and "Thank you, thank you!" Faces wore beaming smiles. People held their fingers up in the V for the victory sign. Some wept. Thousands swarmed into the streets kissing arriving soldiers. Machine guns firing into the air sounded like so many Fourth of July firecrackers. Everywhere the green-white-red-and-black Kuwaiti flag fluttered from buildings, bridges, and hats. A baby dressed in an outfit made from the Kuwaiti flag was held up to be kissed by the liberators. A woman in black robes blew kisses at U.S. Marine lieutenant general Walt Boomer, who rode atop one of the troop carriers. "Makes you appreciate freedom, doesn't it?" he said later.

Somewhere amid all the festival commotion, against the surreal background of billowing black clouds of distant burning oil fields, a lone Kuwaiti quietly pulled an American flag to his lips in salute of this symbol of freedom and the liberation America brought to him and his people.

It was an outburst of exultation that rivaled the liberation of Paris during World War II.[17]

Liberated people celebrate! No one needs to tell them to. They just do it—spontaneously, naturally, with excitement and fervor. Often with wild abandon.

It's no different in the moral/spiritual realm of the life-and-death great controversy that battles around each one of God's people even now. God's liberating work in our lives will always touch an answering chord in our surprised hearts.

Some Jewish writers point to the existential nature of Purim, that it is playtime in Jewish tradition. Such play serves an important existential function. Purim is playing exile. Exile is a basic phenomenon of Jewish existence. It must be grasped existentially, personally, and Purim helps them do that. It enables the Jewish people to remember their double existence in a profoundly personal way.[18] In some way, God's people in every generation must personally connect with the story of Esther—the reality of life and the reality of God *behind the seen,* who will surprise us with His liberating power.

Purim reminds us of the eternal miracle of the survival of God's people.[19] It tells us that when God wins, His people party! What else can they do? And what else is there to do? Such outbursts of joy are acts of worship. What God does is so amazing and mighty. Most important, what God does to preserve His people is not just "back then" for Esther and her people, but now, ongoing—for us!

Also, Purim emphasizes the fact that God's redeemed people must *never lose* their ability to celebrate His goodness and their joy with Him. You can't walk away from such unimaginable liberation and go on with life as usual. All of life must be forever different. Dostoyevsky's experience illustrates it well: I "felt intensely the divine mystery of existence, *the grace of life."* Shouldn't we, too, feel the "grace of life" every moment of our life? Who of us can ever be the same again when the mighty work of Jesus' substitutionary death for our sins has fully sunk in? When it dawns on us that we are free, that we are no longer under condemnation but are a son or daughter of God, how can we walk away from such unimaginable liberation and go on with life as usual? Can we? According to the apostle Paul, it's impossible! "We are ruled by Christ's love for us. . . . Christ did die for all of us. He died so we would no longer live for ourselves, but for the one who died and was raised to life for us" (2 Cor. 5:14, 15, CEV). Hence, he exhorts each one of us to "rejoice in the Lord always; again I will say, rejoice!" (Phil. 4:4). Peter, too, paints an extraordinary picture of our passion for the God *behind the seen* in light of the salvation He has freely brought us in Jesus. "Although you have not seen him, you love him; and even though you do not see him now, you believe in him and rejoice with an indescribable and glorious joy" (1 Peter 1:8, NRSV). And so with

147

Isaiah: "I will rejoice greatly in the Lord, my soul will exult in my God; for He has clothed me with garments of salvation, He has wrapped me with a robe of righteousness" (Isa. 61:10).

Esther and Mordecai wisely gave their people a lasting memorial to God's faithfulness in the feast of Purim. If they had not established an official celebration of Purim, people would have forgotten the events of Esther's lifetime within two or three generations. We must have regular and annual festivities marking God's gracious work in our behalf so that the memory of what He has done will not fade in our minds or those of our children. We who have visited Holocaust memorials know how moving such sites can be. How essential that we remember lest we forget and—perish the thought—live to see such horrors again. "Never again," we say. "Never again."

Human beings need memorials of some kind. Memorials "give the present significance because they give the past perspective."[20] "In order to have perspective, we must have monuments and memorials, places to return to and learn from and talk about and pass on."[21] We must often rehearse the mighty acts of God. Only by maintaining victory through remembrance and celebration can we face the future with faith and hope.

A recurring theme in Esther is that of banquets, drinking parties. In Esther "feasting" has special importance in shaping our reading. The book opens with banquets and closes with a banquet holiday. Banqueting is Esther's defining motif. A motif is a recurrent action, word, event, or object that draws attention to itself and forms linkages that unify a story. By creating cross-connections among passages, motifs help the reader think of one passage in terms of another.[22] Altogether, we find 10 banquets in the story of Esther. They serve as occasions for important events and the transfer of power or as expressions of reality.[23] Interestingly, these 10 banquets are all paired.[24] A suggested pairing of the 10 feasting parties is as follows:

1. The king's banquet for the nobility (Esther 1:2-4) and then his banquet for all the men in Susa (verses 5-8).

2. Vashti's banquet for women (verse 9) and Esther's enthronement banquet (Esther 2:18).

3. The king and Haman's banquet after the decree to destroy the Jews (Esther 3:15) and the Jews' feasting in celebration of Mordecai being honored and the counterdecree (Esther 8:17).

4. Esther's first banquet (Esther 5:4-8), followed by her second banquet (Esther 7:1-9).

5. The first feast of Purim: Adar 14 (Esther 9:17, 19) and the second feast of Purim: Adar 15 (verse 18).

Esther projects four real-to-life contexts in which banqueting takes place—indulgence (Esther 1:3-8), indifference (Esther 3:15), deliverance (Esther 8:17; 9:17-19), and memorial (Esther 9:20-32). It is the last two contexts that Purim commemorates and keeps alive. Deliverance and memorial are both moments when God invites His people of any generation or experience to celebrate His gracious sovereignty in their behalf.

A Forever Party

According to the rabbis, " 'all the festivals will one day cease, but the days of Purim will never cease.' That is, Purim will continue even in the Messianic Age."[25] I find that insight intriguing. It stretches me to reflect on the possibilities of the biblical typology apparent in Purim. I believe the festive atmosphere of God's awesome sovereign grace will ever stir the hearts of God's people through all eternity.

One can only imagine the thrill of joy and celebration when Christ descends "from heaven with a shout, with the voice of the archangel, and with the trump of God" (1 Thess. 4:16, KJV). It is then that the dead in Christ will rise and those who are alive join them in the clouds for that ecstatic moment of meeting with each other and their coming Lord (verses 16, 17). Isaiah gives us words for that glorious moment of meeting: "And it will be said in that day, 'Behold, this is our God for whom we have waited that He might save us. This is the Lord for whom we have waited; let us rejoice and be glad in His salvation'" (Isa. 25:9). Talk about people who think they are dreaming, or about mouths filled with laughter and tongues shouting for joy! The imagery that Psalm 126 portrays will be far surpassed by the final generation of God's people redeemed at the last moment of the darkest hour ever on earth. The return of Jesus will eradicate all doubt that *the God who is now seen* was always there *behind the seen* when we were in crisis on earth. I can hardly wait to see Him! How about you? Only one thing will be appropriate then—a forever party with a Forever Friend. "Amen. Come, Lord Jesus" (Rev. 22:20).

Scripture unequivocally promises that in the end it is God who wins, and when He does, His people party! Light, gladness, joy, and honor will finally and completely and forever fill God's people (Esther 8:16). The grand celebration of God's sovereign work in Esther pulls my mind toward those epochal moments of Revelation that depict shouts of joy because of God's mighty deeds: "And I saw, as it were, a sea of glass mixed with fire, and those who had come off victorious from the beast and from his image and from the number of his name, standing on the sea of glass, holding harps of God. And they sang the song of Moses the bond-servant of God and the song of the Lamb, saying, 'Great and marvelous are Thy works, O Lord God, the Almighty; righteous and true are Thy ways, Thou King of the nations. Who will not fear, O Lord, and glorify Thy name? For Thou alone art holy; for all the nations will come and worship before Thee, for Thy righteous acts have been revealed'" (Rev. 15:2-4).

"Then I saw so many people, no one could count them! They had been taken from every race, tribe, nationality and language and were all dressed in white as they stood in front of the throne and the Lamb, with palm branches in their hands as a sign of their victory. They praised God, saying, 'Our salvation came from the One who sits on the throne and from the Lamb.' Then all the angels, the twenty-four elders and the four living beings fell to their knees, bowed in worship, and praised the One sitting on the throne, saying, 'Amen! Praise, honor, glory, wisdom, thanksgiving, power and might belong to our God forever and ever! Amen!' After this, one of the twenty-four elders came and asked me, 'Do you know who these people are whom you see dressed in white with victory palms in their hands? Do you know where they came from?' I answered, 'Sir, I'm sure you know, but I don't.' He said to me, 'These are people who have come out of great tribulation and have successfully withstood the test of the last days, re-

150

maining loyal to Him who sits on the throne and to the Lamb. They have washed their filthy garments and made them white in the blood of the Lamb. They are dressed in the righteousness of Christ and hold victory palms in their hands. They will stand in the presence of God, because they're God's people. They will serve Him continuously and be with Him in His Temple, and He will be with them and fill their hearts with joy. Never again will they be hungry or thirsty, scorched by the sun or persecuted. The Lamb who is before the throne will be their Shepherd and will feed them. He will lead them to springs of life-giving water, and God Himself will wipe away all tears from their eyes' " (Rev. 7:9-17, Clear Word).

"Blessed and happy are those who have been called and who have accepted God's invitation to the Lamb's wedding and the feast to follow" (Rev. 19:9, Clear Word).

"And the years of eternity, as they roll, will bring richer and still more glorious revelations of God and of Christ. As knowledge is progressive, so will love, reverence, and happiness increase. The more men learn of God, the greater will be their admiration of His character. As Jesus opens before them the riches of redemption and the amazing achievements in the great controversy with Satan, the hearts of the ransomed thrill with more fervent devotion, and with more rapturous joy they sweep the harps of gold; and ten thousand times ten thousand and thousands of thousands of voices unite to swell the mighty chorus of praise. . . . The great controversy is ended. Sin and sinners are no more. The entire universe is clean. One pulse of harmony and gladness beats through the vast creation. From Him who created all flow life and light and gladness, throughout the realms of illimitable space. From the minutest atom to the greatest world, all things, animate and inanimate, in their unshadowed beauty and perfect joy, declare that God is love."[26]

The most amazing part of all this will be the reality that God is no longer *behind the seen*. He will be very much now *the God who is seen—* face-to-face (Rev 22:4). By then everything *behind the seen* will be fully visible. "Now all we can see of God is like a cloudy picture in a mirror. Later we will see him face to face. We don't know everything, but then we will, just as God completely understands us" (1 Cor. 13:12,

CEV). We will have the clearest understanding ever of the moral and spiritual issues involved in the great controversy. God will have fully unmasked sin and evil and forever obliterated them. And the God *behind the seen* will have demonstrated His awesome ability to work all things together for good for those who love Him, trust Him, and find their identity in Him.

Not surprisingly, this now very seen God will also be the God who hosts our grand forever party. Zephaniah proposes one of the most amazing scenes imaginable: "The Lord, your God, is in your midst, a warrior who gives victory; he will rejoice over you with gladness, he will renew you in his love; he will exult over you with loud singing" (Zeph. 3:17, NRSV). The prophet foresees the moment when God rejoices together with them. So decisive is this liberation event that God Himself, the author of joy, joins in with those who now rejoice. It's an incredible anthropomorphic picture.[27] One, though, that captures the heart of Jesus, "who for the joy set before Him endured the cross, despising the shame, and has sat down at the right hand of the throne of God" (Heb. 12:2). Jesus often spoke of this moment of joy, picturing it perhaps best in the imagery of the "waiting Father"[28] who experiences his wildest heartfelt dream when his prodigal son returns home. What does the father do? He throws a party. "Let us eat and be merry," he says (Luke 15:23). "We had to be merry and rejoice," he later adds (verse 32).

Why? I believe it's because God Himself identifies so personally with His people. Identity is a fundamental existential question in Esther. Owning or avoiding one's identity determines who one really is. It shapes the course of history and opens the way to experience God. In the end, God will own those who have chosen by faith to own Him. Revealing Himself in their behalf in a marvelous way, He will come from *behind the seen* to both liberate and forever fellowship with them.

Yes, the rabbis have it right: "All the festivals will one day cease, but the days of Purim will never cease." The experience that the biblical Purim points toward will continue even in the Messianic Age. The redemptive paradigm Esther facilitates will never find closure. The festive atmosphere of God's awesome sovereign grace will ever stir the hearts of His people throughout all eternity. It will be a forever party with a Forever Friend! The measure of love and joy God holds for us is so great that when that forever party takes place, He will rejoice over us with singing.

Oh, how I want to hear Him sing, don't you?

Ruben Alves once noted that "hope is hearing the melody of the future. Faith is to dance to it."[29] Such is the paradigm Esther provides—the melody of the future, the call to begin our dance even now!

[1] E. Peterson, *Five Smooth Stones for Pastoral Work*, p. 158.

[2] Hayyim Schauss, *Guide to Jewish Holy Days: History and Observance* (New York: Schocken Books, 1962), p. 268.

[3] *Ibid.*, p. 267.

[4] Monford Harris, *Exodus and Exile: The Structure of Jewish Holidays* (Minneapolis: Fortress Press, 1992), pp. 96-98.

[5] *Ibid.*

[6] *Ibid.*, p. 98.

[7] Arthur I. Waskow, *Seasons of Our Joy* (New York: Bantam Books, 1982), p. 121.

[8] *Ibid.*, p. 122; Schauss, p. 265.

[9] Waskow, pp. 116, 117.

[10] *Ibid.*, p. 117.

[11] Moshe Braun, *The Jewish Holy Days: Their Spiritual Significance* (Northvale, N.J.: Jason Aronson Inc., 1996), pp. 270, 271.

[12] Harris, pp. 99, 100.

[13] Fyodor Dostoevsky, *Notes From Underground* (New York: Thomas Y. Cromwell Co., 1969), pp. x, xi; Geir Kjetsaa, *Fyodor Dostoyevsky: A Writer's Life* (New York: Viking, 1987), pp. 86-89.

[14] Kjetsaa, p. 88.

[15] Konstantin Mochulsky, *Dostoevsky: His Life and Work* (Princeton University Press, 1967), p. 142.

[16] Peterson, p. 157.

[17] *Time,* Mar. 11, 1991, pp. 38, 39.

[18] Harris, p. 99.

[19] Peterson, p. 158.

[20] C. R. Swindoll, *Esther: A Woman of Strength and Dignity,* p. 182.

[21] *Ibid.*

[22] M. V. Fox, *Character and Ideology in the Book of Esther,* p. 156.

[23] *Ibid.*

[24] *Ibid.*, p. 157.

[25] Waskow, p. 125.

[26] E. G. White, *The Great Controversy,* p. 678.

[27] Mária Eszenyei Széles, *Wrath and Mercy: A Commentary on the Books of Habakkuk and Zephaniah* (Grand Rapids: William B. Eerdmans Pub. Co., 1987), p. 112.

[28] Helmut Thielicke, *The Waiting Father* (New York: Harper & Brothers, 1959), pp. 17-29.

[29] Ruben Alves, *Leadership,* Fall 1988, p. 93.

THE PILGRIM SOUL IN YOU

Esther 10:1-3

T he last three verses of the book of Esther wrap up the story and leave us with both a sense of completion and a realization that life goes on as before in the Medo-Persian Empire: "Now King Ahasuerus laid a tribute on the land and on the coastlands of the sea. And all the accomplishments of his authority and strength, and the full account of the greatness of Mordecai, to which the king advanced him, are they not written in the Book of the Chronicles of the Kings of Media and Persia? For Mordecai the Jew was second only to King Ahasuerus and great among the Jews, and in favor with the multitude of his kinsmen, one who sought the good of his people and one who spoke for the welfare of his whole nation" (Esther 10:1-3).

These three final verses—in fact the final four verses (Esther 9:32-10:3)—form a compelling conclusion. We have the same king, the same kingdom, the same country, and the same capital city. But most of the key players in the story have now faded from our view. Vashti is no longer queen. Haman is gone forever. Since history expects no more greatness from Esther, it appears she returns to a presumably obscure life as queen of the Medo-Persian Empire. Mordecai is alive and well. In the end, only King Ahasuerus and Prime Minister Mordecai remain on-stage. As the curtains close, we see the king levying taxes and using forced labor. By contrast, the book portrays Mordecai as well serving his empire and particularly his own people. The verses reveal a Gentile-ruled, non-God-fearing, oppressive empire in which the people of God live but on which they have little or no lasting impact.[1] True, Mordecai is able to promote the welfare of his own people, but otherwise life goes on as before in the Medo-Persian Empire. Nothing significantly changes in the world. In time he, too, will fade from the scene.

One cannot help wondering about the continued spiritual passion of God's people following the extraordinary events Esther records. Tragically, history reveals that their spiritual focus didn't last—in spite of the many Purims they celebrated in the years that followed. In time God's chosen people drifted once again. It leaves us with the haunting reality of just how difficult it is to keep our heart continually focused on the God who remains *behind the seen*. As life goes on, our vision of God *behind the seen* often fades. It is our nature to live by mere sight!

Esther portrays God's people as being in a less-than-perfect spiritual condition. Thankfully, God has chosen to draw in the Scripture an accurate picture of the history of His people by depicting both their faithful and their unfaithful acts—the book of Esther being an extended example.[2] It shows that "God works providentially on behalf of his people despite their spiritual condition."[3] The book reveals God as actively involved in our lives even when He does not appear to intervene directly. Behind the scenes God works providentially, graciously, sovereignly to reawaken our spiritual passion. To stretch our faith and to push us to own our identity—Him.

Furthermore, Esther reminds us that God is more than sufficient enough to deliver His people from desperate situations. When it comes to the final scene, things turn out right. Events will end well as God wins—always and unequivocally. The promise is that we too can be with Him who wins! "In the end never forget, He wins. Whether you believe it or not, God wins. Whether you accept it or not, God wins. Whether you even return to Him in repentance, God wins. Whether you bow before Him as Savior and Lord, *God still wins.*"[4] The message of Esther is that when He does win, He wants you to be part of His glorious victory.

Where, then, is your heart? What do you see? Whom do you see?

It was December 17, 1941, and Margaret was shaken. Not because the Japanese had bombed Pearl Harbor 10 days earlier but because two young men were madly in love with her and were now vying for her heart. One she had known for years; the other she had met only hours before.

"How can this be happening?" she demanded of the faithless doorkeeper of her heart. It had been all but settled—or so she had thought.

John had given her six years of thoughtful attentiveness, steadfast devotion, and empathetic understanding. The kindest, gentlest man she had ever known, he was the only man more concerned with her inner journey than his own. Poetry was their meat and drink, the medium that intertwined their hearts. Quiet and unassuming, John was tender, understanding, sensitive, sentimental. On a balmy November day on Bandon Beach he shared with her Yeats's haunting poem "When You Are Old."

> "When you are old and gray and full of sleep,
> And nodding by the fire, take down this book,
> And slowly read, and dream of the soft look
> Your eyes had once, and of their shadows deep;
>
> "How many loved your moments of glad grace,
> And loved your beauty with love false or true,
> But one man loved the pilgrim soul in you,
> And loved the sorrows of your changing face."

Pilgrim was ever afterward his pet name for her. She knew without a shadow of a doubt that sometime that coming Christmas he would ask her to marry him.

But all that was yesterday. Now there was Walter, the campus dreamboat her sister had written about and had invited home for Christmas. A gregarious, energetic fellow with rapier-sharp wit, he had an irresistible sense of humor and a winning smile. He had charisma, physical prowess, and passion. When Walter and Margaret first met, it triggered an explosion of awareness. In the days that followed they spoke occasionally to each other in mere words, but almost continually with their eyes. It was as if shock waves surrounded them as the inner spirits of Walter and Margaret challenged each other, communed with each other, longed for each other.

John, so attuned to Margaret's every vibration or nuance, sensed the difference immediately. He could feel her inner spirit withdrawing and was deeply troubled. Even so, Walter knew that only a bold stroke on his part would give him a fighting chance. It was nearing the time

156

for him to return to college—then what? Should he leave without a decision in his favor, John would certainly gain the upper hand again. Margaret's family liked him. Everyone knew it was only a matter of time. He had not a moment to lose. It was the twenty-fourth of December when he made his move. Following breakfast together with the family, he asked Margaret for a couple minutes during which he persuaded her that she owed him a few minutes alone with her. Since they both loved the sea, and since it was an absolutely perfect morning, and since he was leaving so soon, surely she would grant him one small favor: take a short ride to the beach with him.

It was a never-to-be-forgotten Christmas Eve. The couple hours on the beach together that morning soon passed to afternoon and finally evening shadows. When Margaret and Walter finally returned, it was clear to all that her heart had shifted its center of gravity 180 degrees. One moment John represented the perceived future, another moment he did not. Walter had her heart now.

When he realized Walter had one-upped him, John sorrowfully left his parting shot, a single rose on Margaret's dresser with the shortest note he had ever written her:

"December 25, 1941.
"My dearest Margaret,
    "It is clearly over. Yet, if you should change your mind, just send me a red rose, signing the card 'Pilgrim,' and I shall come to you if it be in my power to do so.

"I shall always love you.
"John"

Margaret and Walter were married the first day of May. The years swept by on winged feet, 43 years of happiness filled with perpetual adventure, good fortune, travel, splendid homes, villas, mountain resorts—and love. Then Walter took ill and died. Now Margaret was alone.

Several years of loneliness passed, then unexpectedly Margaret ran into John at a family celebration in distant California. It was the first she had seen or even heard anything of him in nearly 47 years. There he was with his wife. Suddenly memories flooded back upon her. Something stirred deep within. The realization that after all those years the fire still burned now shook her.

She returned to her life, only now lonelier than ever. Now she yearned—she longed—for John. But now . . . it was too late. Then one November morning in 1991 she received a chatty little note from her daughter that included some unexpected news: "By the way, just heard that the wife of your old sweetheart died of cancer. A year ago, I believe." Now there was no longer any human barrier separating her from John. But would he, after all these years, still be interested in her? Would he so resent her rejection of him that he'd refuse to have anything to do with her? After almost a half century, could he possibly still care for her in the old way?

"Mother, didn't he leave any ragged edges—any open ends you could take advantage of?" her daughter asked one day? "Or was it a surgical cut—" She stopped suddenly as Margaret's hands flew to her face.

"Mother, what is it?"

"Oh, I just remembered . . . no, it was anything but a surgical cut. How could I have possibly forgotten! He . . . he . . . uh . . . left me a rose the morning he left, Christmas morning. What a present! I cried like I never had before, or have since. A rose . . . and . . . a note."

"Go on. Go on!" her daughter commanded. So Margaret opened her heart and told all about John, the love of her youth, including her pet name "Pilgrim."

On the twenty-first day of December, 1991, the doorbell rang and a florist delivery boy handed John a slim package. His eyes widened with disbelief as he read the message on the card. It consisted of one word: "Pilgrim." The back of the card contained no name—but it did have an address and phone number.

On the twenty-third day of December Margaret held three perfect red roses in her hand. On a small sheet of stationery were the words:

"Dearest Pilgrim,

"Second Rose received; am returning. First Rose long since dead;

158

am sending replacement. Third Rose to present my case—and Emily:
> "Where Roses would not dare to go,
> What Heart would risk the way—
> And so I send my Crimson Scouts
> To sound the Enemy—"

"If they are persuasive enough, I'll see you at Bandon Beach, December 25, 9:00 a.m., in vicinity of Yeats Sand Dune.

"Until then—
"Your John"

Christmas morning on Bandon Beach a tall graceful woman descended the stairs leading down to the beach at exactly 9:00 a.m.. The roses of youth were in her cheeks, and pinned to her breast was a corsage of three crimson roses.

At the bottom of the stairs, she kicked off her shoes. After rounding the huge rock, she saw him, standing by a sand dune that looked vaguely familiar.

When she got close enough to read his eyes—
and see his open arms—
she broke into a run.

Pilgrim had come home.[5]

Esther speaks to the "pilgrim soul" in every one of us. It reminds us that our heart, that unpredictable entity within us, can so easily shift its center of gravity 180 degrees from the living God to the enchanting world we see around us. But it also points to the unseen God who graciously works and quietly waits *behind the seen* for us to return to Him fully and forever!

> "Long years apart—can make no
> Breach a second cannot fill—
> The absence of the Witch does not
> Invalidate the spell—

> "The embers of a Thousand Years

Uncovered by the Hand
That fondled them when they were Fire
Will stir and understand."
                                    —Emily Dickinson

No matter how long it's been, God can rekindle the flame! He can renew our spiritual passion. It can be your experience—"The embers of a thousand years uncovered by the hand that fondled them when they were fire will stir and understand."

Such is the heartfelt theme of Esther. God is waiting, working. For you. Your very life depends on the enduring quality of your relationship with Him. Let the pilgrim soul in you gaze with wonder *behind the seen*. Experience the God whose gracious love and awesome power are at work for you. Choose Him. Once and for all, take a stand. Now. Today! Own your identity in Him.

———————

[1] A. B. Luter and B. C. Davis, *God Behind the Seen,* p. 360.

[2] *Ibid.,* p. 364.

[3] *Ibid.,* p. 366.

[4] C. R. Swindoll, *Esther: A Woman of Strength and Dignity,* p. 194.

[5] Adapted from Joe L. Wheeler, "The Third Rose," *Christmas in My Heart,* vol. 3, pp. 109–125.